Praise Above All

Praise Above All

Discovering the Welsh Tradition

A. M. ALLCHIN

UNIVERSITY OF WALES PRESS
CARDIFF
1991

British Library Cataloguing in Publication Data
Allchin, A. M. (Arthur Macdonald), *1930–*
    Praise above all
    1. Welsh Poetry, *special subjects. Christianity*
    I. Title
    891.661209382
    ISBN 0-7083-1091-5

The publishers wish to acknowledge the financial assistance of the Welsh Arts Council towards the costs of producing this volume.

Typeset by Megaron, Cardiff
Jacket design by Ruth Dineen
Printed in the United Kingdom by Bookcraft, Midsomer Norton

For James and Stevie
with love and gratitude

Beth yw byw? Cael neuadd fawr
Rhwng cyfyng furiau.

(Waldo Williams)

Contents

Acknowledgements

In the writing of such a book as this which is full of the words and thoughts of other people, the author incurs innumerable debts. I cannot hope to mention all those who have helped me on the way into the discovery of Wales. To all I am grateful. Two friends and teachers who are now dead, must however be mentioned, Herbert Hodges and Idris Foster. Among the living I think in the first place of the translators of Welsh verse and specially of Tony Conran and Joseph Clancy, and then of friends and colleagues in the Welsh Department of University College, Bangor, and in particular of the head of the department, Bedwyr Lewis Jones, and of Derec Llwyd Morgan, who was director of the Wales Research Centre at the time when I spent a term in Bangor in the summer of 1988.

I am grateful to the staff of the University of Wales Press and especially to Ned Thomas, Susan Jenkins and Esyllt Penri for much invaluable help in preparing the book for publication, and to Robert Farmer for making the index. I am also grateful to the many poets and publishers who have granted permission for me to quote extensively from their works. Acknowledgement to these sources is given in the notes.

The title of this book contains a reference to a great praise poem of the eighteenth century, Christopher Smart's *A Song to David*.

> Praise above all-for praise prevails
> Heap up the measure, load the scales,
>   And good to goodness add:
> The gen'rous soul her saviour aids
> But peevish obloquy degrades;
>   The Lord is great and glad.

Foreword

In one of his rare English essays, Saunders Lewis describes a poem of congratulation written in the last years of the eighteenth century to a south Welsh country gentleman, Thomas Lloyd, the squire of Cwmgloyn in north Pembrokeshire. The poem is written to mark the occasion of the launching of a new ship built for the Lloyd family at the little port of Trefdraeth (Newport). It is the work of a local poet, Ioan Siencyn, whose name has not otherwise been remembered in the history of Welsh literature. Yet, Saunders Lewis maintains, this poem is a not unworthy successor to the professional praise poetry of the medieval bards. Ioan Siencyn is heir to a tradition which is more than a thousand years old, and he writes with an unselfconscious awareness of the continuity of that tradition.

'There, I think, we capture something essential in the progress of Welsh poetry. We call it the literary tradition of Wales. It means you cannot pluck a flower of song off a headland in Dyfed (south-west Wales) in the late eighteenth century without stirring a great northern star of the sixth century. And all the inter-mediaries are involved. The fourteenth century gave the technique of *dyfalu* or image making, the sixteenth century brought in the Vergilian echoes, the seventeenth century gave the measure. The whole body of Welsh poetry from the sixth century onwards has contributed directly to Ioan Siencyn's verses.' All this is true in the case of an almost forgotten poet, revealing as it does, 'the nature and continuity of the Welsh poetic tradition . . . and its quality and creative virtue: for the virtue of the tradition is that it may enable a quite minor poet to write a major poem'.[1]

   An English or American reader coming across this passage for
the first time is likely to be struck by its assertion of the continuity
of tradition in the literary world of Wales. But he may well
wonder whether the tradition is still alive today, and how far
indeed it was really alive at the end of the eighteenth century. Was
Ioan Siencyn simply the last rustic survivor of an ancient culture
finally running out of steam? Another notable Welsh scholar
comments on this very poem, 'Bardic allegiance to noble families
persisted in a debased form well into the eighteenth century'.[2] Is
this the last echo of the poetry in praise of the nobility which had
rung out so clearly four centuries before?

   It so happens that we can give from the very same decade, and
from a very different part of Wales, examples of other poets which
will show that the point which Saunders Lewis is making is
anything but a marginal one. In 1793 Thomas Jones of Denbigh
wrote a poem to the song thrush. The poem and its writer are both
of exceptional interest. Thomas Jones was the leading scholar and
intellectual of the second generation of Welsh Methodism, a
movement which at the end of the eighteenth century was
spreading rapidly through north Wales. He came from a family of
the gentry, and unlike the majority of his class, he had thrown in
his lot with the new radical movement of his times, the
Methodists. His was a family which had had its own tradition of
patronage of the bards. Most of Thomas Jones's work lies in the
field of theology and church history; he was in his own way, an
extremely learned man, and a great Evangelical. He was also a
fine writer of strongly doctrinal hymns. But in 1793, he chose to
compose a poem – it covers some seven pages – in praise of the
thrush, which both in its style and its content might belong to the
fourteenth century. It is as if Charles Wesley or Charles Simeon
had been able to compose in the manner and spirit of Chaucer or
Langland. This is a poem which will be considered in more detail
later in this book. Suffice it to say now that it is a poem which I do
not think could have been written at the end of the eighteenth
century in any of the other major European languages. It is not a
pastiche, nor even an imitation of a medieval model. It is a living
expression of a tradition which has crossed the watershed of the
Renaissance and the Reformation, not without being deeply

influenced by them, but without losing its own sense of inward continuity.

In 1793 when Thomas Jones wrote this poem, a girl of seventeen was coming to maturity in a farmhouse in the hills of north Wales, not so very far from Denbigh where his family had its seat. Ann Griffiths (at that date she was known by her maiden name, Nansi Thomas), unlike Thomas Jones, had the advantage neither of a formal education nor of birth into a family of the gentry. Unlike Ioan Siencyn she had had little or no training in the traditional techniques of the bardic schools. But she was a woman touched by an uncommon genius. She is by common consent the finest woman poet in the whole tradition of Wales. In the brief years between 1797 and her death in 1805 she was to produce a group of hymns which, while they lack the formal marks of continuity with the earlier centuries which are to be seen in the work of Thomas Jones or Ioan Siencyn, none the less strike us forcibly as the products of a long history. They are cast in the relatively simple metrical forms employed by the Methodist hymn-writers in the previous fifty years. But in them, one is also conscious of the presence of a tradition, in this case the universal tradition of Christian faith and worship, in all its height and depth, its length and breadth. Something of the classical utterance of the praise of God which we find in the writings of the Fathers both in east and west comes to new birth here in this north Montgomeryshire farmhouse. We see again, in a different form, evidence of the strength and vitality of the tradition of Wales of which she was a part.

Twenty years ago when I first became aware of the hymns and letters of Ann Griffiths, through translations made by the late Professor Hodges, I was astonished by the sense which they conveyed of standing within a strong tradition of faith and understanding. As we began to explore their unexpected riches, Herbert Hodges and I constantly asked ourselves, 'How can these things be?' There was something which seemed inexplicable in these verses, not only in the sense that genius is something which always baffles our powers of explanation, but in the sense that this young woman, in an isolated farmhouse in the foothills of the Berwyn, seemed to be the representative of an imperial tradition.

I think, now that I have entered a little further into the Welsh heritage, that I can see more how that was. Ann stands beside Thomas Jones and Ioan Siencyn – they are in some ways incongruous companions – as a representative of a tradition which has brought down till today, a living sense of the presence of the past and of the nearness of eternity, a tradition which centres on the practice of praise. It will be the purpose of this book to explore the way in which that tradition, alive at the end of the eighteenth century and still alive today, gives us access to areas of our shared Christian and pre-Christian inheritance which are not otherwise available.

In these pages, therefore, we shall explore the theme of praise, as it is found in the Welsh poetic tradition from the beginning till today. The first half of the book gives a rapid, general overview of the whole tradition and is intended especially as an introduction to the subject for those to whom it is wholly or almost wholly new. In the second part of the book there are more detailed studies of aspects of this theme, particularly in relation to the writing of the last two centuries. Here I have tried to develop contrasts and comparisons between the Welsh tradition and that of other nations, so that we may perceive its own specific quality in a European and indeed a more than European context.

Whereas in the first part of the book I have kept the quotation of Welsh words and phrases to an absolute minimum, in the second part I have quite often cited the original as well as the translation. I hope that this will be of interest to those who are unfamiliar with the language and of help to those who are already familiar with it.

I

The Tradition Surveyed

To Recreate an Unblemished World: the earliest Welsh poetry

The practice of praise stands at the heart of the Welsh poetic tradition, and the purpose of praise, as Waldo Williams (1904–71) put it, is 'to recreate an unblemished world'. What is true of the Welsh tradition is true of the Celtic world as a whole. Indeed in some sense the practice of praise is essential to all poetry, whatever nation or culture it comes from. This is particularly the case when our human life is seen in the perspective of the life of God. As David Jones remarks, 'if poetry is praise, as prayer is, it can never coexist with any malignant and persistent criticism of the nature of things – however much, surprisingly, the poet be a master grouser, his theme a complaint, his mood dejected'.[1] In such a perspective, praise and thanksgiving become the dominant notes in our attitudes towards our life in this world, seen as God's gift. But it is significant that this comment should come from an Anglo-Welsh writer, exceptionally conscious of the meaning of the Welsh tradition.

This primacy of praise is something of a problem in our society. Today the writer's task seems often to be conceived as one of belittling rather than enhancing the significance of the subject he is discussing. It is a time in which reductive analysis, 'explaining away', seems more in demand than admiration or appreciation. The praise of the great is for us an acute problem. We have seen too much of it in totalitarian societies. Joseph Clancy comments on this in the introduction to his volume of translations of medieval Welsh verse: 'What self-respecting modern poet, as his chief task, eulogizes the dean of a college, the bishop of a diocese, the local captain of industry, the mayors of various cities, and the president or prime minister of his country?'[2] Yet praise of such figures as these made up a large part of the work of the Welsh poets of the Middle Ages.

I

It will be the thesis of this book that our problem about praise arises in the end from the fact that we no longer see it in its religious context, and therefore do not recognize the deep roots from which it springs, nor the final goal to which it tends. Praise, like all worship, with which it is so closely allied, is that which is due to God. All other forms of praise directly, or more often indirectly, refer back to him. It is in this context that we begin to see how the practice of praise can be said to 'recreate an unblemished world'. By referring all things back to their creator we see them again lit up by the light of his glory, shot through with the energies of his wisdom and his love. We see that unblemished world of origins, in which God saw all that he had made, and behold it was very good.

Our twentieth-century aversion to praising our fellow men and women is in large measure a consequence of our failure to see this. The banal and idolatrous praises which the dictators of our time have demanded and encouraged rightly repel and appal us. In an avowedly atheist society, the practice of praise, and of poetry as a whole, becomes increasingly impossible, loses all meaning. It cannot by definition be referred back, however indirectly, to the one to whom praise is due. It is very striking how strong and clear are the religious affirmations of the great Russian poets of the middle of this century. When confronted with the particular horror of the cult of personality surrounding Stalin, Pasternak, Akhmatova, and Mandelstam (none of them conventionally 'religious' people) are all united in this. The poetic act is ultimately a religious act, a sacred act. This is why it is felt to be subversive in such a society.

The well-known words of Dylan Thomas in the foreword to his *Collected Poems* (1952) are also striking in this context, coming to us from a world which while not explicitly atheist constantly denies God in the ordering of its priorities, 'These poems . . . were written for the love of Man and in praise of God, and I would be a

damn fool if they weren't'.[3] Praise of man when not seen in this
light takes on a repulsive, servile tone. Praise of God is something
different. Philip Toynbee makes this point with emphasis. 'True
praise of God is quite unlike praising a powerful human being. Far
from abasing ourselves in order to flatter the emperor by
proclaiming how high he is above us, our adoration of God should
be a means of bringing us closer to him. The purer our praise the
more we ourselves are filled with the God we are praising.'[4]

This is a vital insight into the nature of the praise of God. It is an
activity which far from demeaning the one who takes part in it,
actually lifts him up, associates him with the one who is praised,
and so brings the two together in a shared life. Once this is seen to
be the very nature of the praise of God, and once the absolute
priority of this praise over all other forms is acknowledged, then
we find that the other forms themselves need no longer be seen as
demeaning or degrading. In the medieval Welsh poetic textbooks, for instance, it is prescribed that a song of praise of God
shall be sung before all other songs. All other persons and things
are to be praised in due proportion and order, in relation to him.
As a result of this the medieval court poet in no way feels himself
subservient to the prince he praises. There is a reciprocal
relationship between them. The poet gives the prince the honour
which is due to him. He increases his capacity to fulfil the role
which he has been called to play and to embody the virtues which
are attributed to him. He gives the prince the promise that his
memory will continue beyond the boundary of death. But at the
same time the poet receives honour, protection and rewards from
the prince. Without him, the poet is nothing. With him, he is his
companion. Indeed at certain times in the bardic poetry of
Ireland we find that the poet thinks of himself as the prince's wife,
so close is the relationship between them.

When the practice of praise is seen as rooted in the praise of
God, then other forms of praise cease to be idolatrous. This
reference back to the praise of God need not be explicit or even
conscious. Very often it is implicit and assumed. But in such a
context all acts of praise acquire a certain sacred character. They
are acts which bring together the person who praises with the one
who is praised, in a movement in which God himself is at least

implicitly concerned, and in which something of his goodness and
glory is revealed.

To praise another human being or any part of God's creation
means to recognize, to celebrate and to proclaim the goodness
which is in them. All goodness comes from God, and is a sign of his
presence in the world that he has made. When we praise what is
good, whatever it may be, we enter into communion with it and
enhance its goodness by giving it new expression. This is true
whether we praise a child or a tree, a star or a house, a nation or a
family. In and through the created goodness which we name and
rejoice in, we are rejoicing in the uncreated energies of the divine
wisdom and the divine love. All these forms of praise are the
infinitely varied manifestations of that disinterested joy, that
delighted wonder in all that is shining and beautiful, which is at
the heart of worship and adoration. To praise what is not good, in
servile or fearful flattery, is indeed to degrade and demean both
the one who praises and the one who is praised. There is nothing of
this in the praise and worship of God. Falling down before him we
are lifted up. The saints grow taller when they kneel.

Seen in this perspective the task of the priest and the task of the
poet are very closely allied. Both are called, in different ways, to
bless; and to bless (*benedicere*) in its original meaning is to speak
good things, to declare the goodness which is latent in the world
around us, when that world is seen and known as the world of
God. Both are called to offer up a sacrifice of praise and
thanksgiving and, as Augustine makes plain, a sacrifice is any
action in which things are made over to God, restored to him, so
that from his uncreated holiness their own created holiness may
be made manifest and renewed. It is striking how persistent is this
thought of the sacrifice of praise and thanksgiving in the
celebration of the Eucharist, the central act of Christian worship.
Before and behind all the many controversies about the sacrificial
nature of the rite, there is this common recognition that this action
whose very name signifies thanksgiving is to be understood as a
sacrifice of praise. The celebration of this rite, which is entrusted
in a special way to the one who is called to be a priest, is thus
closely linked with the work and activity of the poet; however
little this fact may at times be recognized on either side of the

equation. And this work of blessing and offering, which is at once priestly and prophetic, and which belongs in a special way to those who enter on a priestly calling or practise a poetic craft, in reality belongs to all men and women by reason of the humanity which they share. This is a major part of what we mean when we say that we are created in God's image and likeness. We share in his creative work.

Some of the early Christian writers love to speak of man as created as a priest and a king, given dominion over God's creation not in order to exploit and oppress it, but so as to articulate and develop the song of praise which it presents, hidden in all things, animate and inanimate. We could say as truly that man is called to be a priest and a poet, one who under God and with God is called to be a creator. This is the meaning of the word *poietes* in the original Greek, just as it is the meaning of the medieval English word for poet, *maker*. In artistic creativity, we seem to come nearer to God's own gift of creation *ex nihilo* than at any other time. Not, of course, that the human maker is ever altogether independent of the material which he uses, and the tradition which he inherits. But would it not be true to say of *King Lear*, of Beethoven's *Ninth Symphony*, or of Andrei Rublyov's icon of the Holy Trinity, that in some very radical way they were not there, could not be imagined before they were created? In them something genuinely new has come into existence.

What is true supremely of such supreme acts of human making is true also in its own degree of a great variety of acts which demand both skill and application and a certain degree of that gift which we call inspiration. Here the material with which we work is more obviously important, and the tradition within which we work more evidently of vital significance. Yet each act of creation is in some sense new, and the greatest works of art are born within a tradition to which many lesser works have contributed. There is something sacred, something of the paradoxically transcendent in each true work of art. As the Australian poet Les Murray remarks,

If a poem is real, it is inexhaustible; it cannot be summarised or transposed into other words . . . It is marked by a strange simultaneity of stillness and racing excitement . . . Each time we return, the poem is the same, and yet fresh intimations of significance are likely to rise from it. It is, as St Thomas said, *radiant*. And we can grow in relation to it, perhaps over our whole lifetime, if it is a favourite poem. It is complete, finite, yet inexhaustible.'[5]

It is one of the particular joys of meeting with the Welsh-speaking world to find a society in which making poems is still regarded as an ordinary occupation, in which there seems to be no absolute discontinuity, though there is a very great difference of degree, between the kind of versifying which has a good deal in common with the solving of a crossword puzzle to the writing of a work of classical inspiration. In the English-speaking world unfortunately, the writing of poetry has come to be thought of as so special, so marginal, so extraordinary, that it becomes important for us to stress the lines of continuity which run from all forms of what we call artistic creation to acts of making of a more obviously everyday character, the creation of a garden, the cooking of a good meal, the playing of a game of rugby. In all these activities, when well done, something is made, an object or an event, which reveals a little of things as they were meant to be; in other words which shows us the glory of the world. Here there is the 'recreation of an unblemished world'. The spontaneous roar of the crowd in the sports stadium at the unlooked-for goal, the standing ovation at the end of the concert, the unpremeditated gasp of pleasure at the dish set down on the table, all these acts of praise are acts which recognize, celebrate and proclaim some tiny revelation of the rightness of things. We have some awareness of wholeness, a glimpse of God's glory.

As poets, all human beings are called to be co-workers with God, co-creators. We are called to discern and proclaim the latent goodness of the creation around us and within us. As priests we are called to offer that goodness back to God in a movement of praise and thanksgiving, which is at the same time a movement of intercession and concern. So it is that Waldo Williams can sing of his mother, the wife of a primary schoolteacher in a Pembrokeshire village, 'she recreated with his praise an un-blemished world'.[6] The final suggestion of the poem is that she made of her life an offering of prayer and praise in which joy and grief were so woven together as to be a divine clothing, an offering in which the priesthood of her concern was spread as a protecting veil over the daily cares and achievements of the society in which she lived.

II

The themes which we have been outlining so far are ones which we shall find recurring again and again in the poetic tradition of Wales, and of the Celtic world as a whole, from pre-Christian times until today. They receive notable expression in a mid-thirteenth-century Irish poem which is written in defence of poetry, in reply to a priest who claimed to have come from Rome with a letter condemning the Irish bardic schools. The writer refuses to believe that such a message can be genuine.

> But you were not told in Rome
> to banish bards, my priest.
> In some non-Rome or other
> you got that foolish instruction.

He goes on to assert that a poem is *Donum Dei*, a gift of God, clearly implying the divine origin of poetic inspiration. A poem needs to be recognized as such, and the poet as a professional rightly claims his payment for it, he argues. Neither Patrick nor Columba banished poets from Ireland. Indeed he asserts that Columba came to their defence.

> To praise man is to praise
> the One who made him,
> and man's earthly possessions
> add to God's mighty praise.

> All metre and mystery
> touch on the Lord at last.
> The tide thunders ashore
> in praise of the High King.

It would be difficult to express more clearly the conviction which lies at the heart of the praise poetry of Ireland and Wales alike. All in the end returns to God. Moreover for the poet, as for the priest, praise and remembrance, *eucharist* and *anamnesis* lie very close together.

> If poetry went, my people,
> man's knowledge would reach back
> no further than his father . . . [7]

The whole complex web of relationships linking generation to generation would be broken. The celebration of the great deeds of the past, both tragic and heroic would be lost. These are the things which lie in the poet's domain.

This poem is not only or even primarily a protest against the centralizing power of Rome. It is a protest against a whole Christian culture, Latin and to some degree Greek, which rather sharply divides sacred from secular, priestly from poetic, grace from nature and God from humanity, on behalf of a world view which sees these things as very closely interrelated in ways which sometimes fascinate us and sometimes disconcert us. It would not be true to say that the Celtic tradition, at least in its Christian guise, simply identifies the one realm with the other or breaks down all distinction between them. The Celtic writers are not pantheists; they do not confuse creation with the Creator. But they are frequently panentheist. They see all things in God and God in all things.

This is undoubtedly one of the reasons for the widespread interest in Celtic Christianity which is evident today. We have lived through a period of some centuries in which western Christianity, both Catholic and Protestant, has tended to harden these distinctions between divine and human and make them into separations. The religion of redemption seems to have become divorced from the religion of creation, and sometimes completely to have overshadowed it. Christianity which is a religion of incarnation seems to have become curiously disembodied, and more and more restricted to a narrowly religious sphere. In a situation such as this there is an instinctive turning towards the tradition of the Celtic Christian world which offers us a different picture of things, a picture in which the whole creation is seen as touched by God and full of God. In it the praise and glory of God become embodied in strong and startingly sensuous ways.

We see this quality when we turn to two of the earliest religious texts to be found in Welsh, the ninth-century verses from the Juvencus manuscript in Cambridge and the better-known lines which probably date from the following century, 'Glorious Lord I give you greeting'.

> Almighty Creator, who hast made all things,
> The world cannot express all thy glories,
> Even though the grass and the trees should sing.
>
> The Father has wrought so great a multitude of wonders
> That they cannot be equalled.
> No letters can contain them, no letters can express them.
>
> He who made the wonder of the world
> Will save us, has saved us.
> It is not too great toil to praise the Trinity.
>
> Purely, humbly, in skilful verse
> I should delight to give praise to the Trinity.
> It is not too great toil to praise the Son of Mary.[8]

In this poem it is clear that creation and redemption are brought very close together. In an alternative translation Dr Enid Pierce Roberts writes, 'It is the Man who created the wonder of the world who will save us, who has saved us' therefore 'no labour is too great to praise the Trinity'.[9] The creative Word is also the redemptive Word, one of the Holy Trinity made flesh for us, become the Son of Mary. It is clear that all creation is caught up into the praise of God, the leaves on the trees, the very blades of grass. Therefore for man it is not too great toil, no labour is too great, to praise the Holy Trinity. It is very interesting to note that the word translated labour or toil, *gnif* occurs in another poem of the same period but of a very different kind. This is a poem which reflects a pre-Christian view of the inevitable, ineluctable character of fate. There man's life is spoken of as 'a long toil with no deliverance from weariness'. Here the darkness of the pre-Christian world with its sense of human life as held in the grip of an iron unyielding destiny gives way to the light of another hope, another expectation. In praising God, human life is drawn into communion with the one who is Lord and Giver of life, here and in the world to come.

When we turn from this poem to 'Glorious Lord, I give you greeting', our first impression may be one of confusion. Again there can be no question but that all things are called to praise God. But at first sight they seem to be jumbled together, natural objects, human artefacts, inner thoughts, outer actions, the heroes of Israel's faith. Then perhaps we begin to ask whether we have here an equivalent to the sinuous, spiral lines to be found in Celtic manuscript illuminations. There is a pattern, but it is other than we had expected it to be. What is unquestionable is that all things, Old Testament and New, inner world and outer, gifts of creation, gifts of redemption come together in a single focus.

> Glorious Lord, I give you greeting!
> Let the church and the chancel praise you,
> Let the chancel and the church praise you,
> Let the plain and the hill-side praise you,
> Let the world's three well-springs praise you,
> Two above wind and one above land,
> Let the dark and the daylight praise you.
> Abraham, founder of the faith, praised you:
> Let the life everlasting praise you,
> Let the birds and the honeybees praise you,
> Let the shorn stems and the shoots praise you.
> Both Aaron and Moses praised you:
> Let the male and the female praise you,
> Let the seven days and the stars praise you,
> Let the air and the ether praise you,
> Let the books and the letters praise you,
> Let the fish in the swift streams praise you,
> Let the thought and the action praise you,
> Let the sand-grains and the earth-clods praise you,
> Let all the good that's performed praise you.

> And I shall praise you, Lord of glory:
> Glorious Lord, I give you greeting![10]

The close juxtaposition which we find in this poem of church and chancel, and plain and hillsides, books and letters, birds and honey-bees can be paralleled in a group of poems from the same period in Ireland. These are the hermit poems which come from a movement of monastic reform, the Culdee movement, which took place in the ninth century. They celebrate the life of one who goes out into the woodland to live either alone, or with a small group of disciples, a life of simplicity and prayer and silence. With their delighted celebration of the beauty of nature some centuries before the time of St Francis these poems are sometimes said to have a Franciscan quality. They remind us that Francis was not alone in seeing the hand of God in all things.

> O Son of the living God
> ancient, eternal king,
> grant me a hidden hut
> to be my home in the wild,
>
> with green shallow water
> running by its side,
> and a clear pool to wash off sin
> by grace of the Holy Ghost;
>
> a lovely wood close by
> around it on every hand
> to feed the birds of many voices
> to shelter them and hide;
>
> southward facing for warmth
> with a stream in its grounds
> and choice land of thick growth
> good for every crop;

The poet goes on to pray that God will send him some disciples:

> six pairs besides myself
> gathered all about me

praying for all eternity
to the King who lights the Sun;

a lovely church, with linen
a home for Heaven's King,
with bright lamps shining down
on the clear bright Scriptures.[11]

These clear bright Scriptures, the illuminated manuscripts of the Gospels and the Psalter are some of the finest master-pieces of Celtic art. They suggest to us two of the sources of this vision of a clear, transfigured world. One is to be found in the Gospels themselves, in the words which Jesus uses about the material world, the world of plants and animals, in his parables and in his teaching in the sermon on the mount. The other is to be discovered in the Psalms, and in the way in which they speak about the glory of God as revealed in his creation. Here is a source whose importance should not be underestimated. The constant, daily recitation of the Psalms constituted the substance of monastic prayer in the Celtic world no less than in the world of Latin, Greek or Syriac Christianity. The men who wrote the hermit poems of ninth-century Ireland were men who from their youth would have known the whole psalter by heart.

A monastic writer of our own day, who was also a considerable poet, Thomas Merton, reminds us of this. 'The psalms are perhaps the most significant and influential collection of religious poems ever written.'[12] The Old Testament writers had wholly rejected any suggestion that the natural world was divine in itself. They were repelled by idolatry. But this did not make their vision of the world a godless one. 'The men who wrote the psalms were carried away in an ecstasy of joy, when they saw God in the cosmic symbolism of his created universe.'[13] Freed from the sense of being imprisoned in the material world, they were liberated to see traces of God's glory everywhere at work in it.

Creation had been given to men as a clear window through which the light of God would shine into men's souls. Sun and moon, night and day, rain and sun, the cross, the flowering tree, all these things were transparent. They spoke to man not of themselves, but of him who made them.[14]

At the time when Merton wrote these words he was immersed in the daily recitation of the Psalms in the monastic choir. He was constantly making the psalmist's experience his own. We shall find echoes of his words as we follow the development of the poetic tradition in Wales. In their celebration of the beauty and translucence of the natural world, the poets of Wales have been more biblical than some of those who have studied them have been willing to allow.

2

Mirrors Of The Eternal: from Dafydd Ap Gwilym to Thomas Jones

Three centuries or more after the poems we have been considering were composed, in the period which followed the defeat and death of the last native Prince of Wales in 1282, we come to the poet who is recognized as one of the greatest of the poets of Wales, Dafydd ap Gwilym (1320–70).

Dafydd's reputation is not altogether easily understood from outside the world of Welsh culture and language. His poetry is, even by Welsh standards, remarkably difficult to translate, so that it is hard to get the measure of it in any language other than the original. There are other reasons for this difficulty. For a great poet, Dafydd's output is not very large. Some 150 poems, none particularly long, written in a limited number of metrical forms. At first sight they may seem somewhat repetitious. The theme of the love tryst, successful or more often unsuccessful, is repeated in many variations. Only gradually does the nature of their variety and inventiveness become apparent. Only gradually does the non-Welsh reader begin to realize their subtlety, their strength, and their varied excellence.

Dafydd has it in common with his near contemporary, Geoffrey Chaucer, that he is an extremely sophisticated poet, whose work is full of an irony and humour, which across the centuries is not always easy to catch. The shades of meaning in his poems are very delicate. Have we been able to catch the tone of his voice, to hear what he is saying? There is ample room for disagreement amongst his commentators.

This is particularly the case with his attitude towards religious questions, as we find it not so much in the small group of his directly religious poems as in his work as a whole. Most are agreed that the religious poems are sincere statements of a regular medieval believer. But in his attitude towards the representatives of the church, particularly the friars of his time, his position is much more ambiguous. Certainly he is at odds with the medieval church's standards of sexual morality.

All are agreed again that Dafydd has a great capacity for self mockery. He frequently makes fun of himself, of his misadventures in love, of his failures to reach his desired objective. We shall see a striking example of this quality in the first poem we shall examine. All are agreed too that Dafydd's poetry contains a delighted praise of nature, particularly of the woodland in spring and summer-time, and of the birds which are part of that world. There is something here beyond the ordinary medieval delight in the coming of spring, something which we may feel is in line with that love of nature which we have seen in the earlier poetry of Wales and of Ireland. The continental scholar Theodore Chotzen remarks,

> It is precisely this feeling for nature which gives the poetry of the Celtic peoples a special place in medieval literature. The poems of Dafydd ap Gwilym above all abound in striking small features which only the expert eye of an attentive observer and of a great lover of nature would have been able to grasp.[1]

Dafydd's poems about the birds, the lark, the thrush, the nightingale, the blackbird, do not deal in vague generalities. The birds are observed in all their particularity.

One of the chief characteristics of these verses in praise of nature is the way in which in them Dafydd makes constant use of the vocabulary of Christian worship to speak of natural phenomena. The most striking example of this is in the poem known as 'The Mass in the Grove', one of the most translated and anthologized of all his verses.[2] What are we to make of this constant interplay between the vocabulary of grace and the vocabulary of nature? Are we to see in these poems works which are basically pagan in feeling and outlook, which the poet has adorned with a free and irreverent use of sacred and liturgical imagery? Or are we to say that, in these poems, the language of creation and the language of redemption have been brought together into a new and remarkable unity?

I

Before we come to tackle this question directly let us look again at the poems which are full of mockery and humour. Dafydd often holds together within the same poem the language of praise and the language of satire. This in itself need not surprise us. Praise and satire have always lived together in close juxtaposition in Celtic art. If we praise the goodness of things or persons in the context of a vision of their ideal, or even their divine splendour it is impossible not to recognize also the incongruities, the dissonances, the inadequacies which in our actual experience of life so often break in upon that ideal. Indeed the more we glimpse the glory of things on the one side, the more we shall see the contrasting darkness on the other. For we do not live in an ideal world, and our daily experience of life is frequently one of the disparity, sometimes painful, sometimes comic, sometimes both, between man's pretensions to the divine and his actual performance.

It is part of the greatness of Dafydd that he handles this theme with such ability and vigour. Nowhere is this more the case than in the poem called 'Trouble at the Tavern'. The poet comes to a tavern in the town, possibly one of those border towns, Wrexham or Oswestry, where Welsh and English lived uneasily together. He spies a beautiful girl, orders a good dinner with a bottle of wine, invites her to join him, and promises himself to come to visit her once all the rest of the company are in bed. Unfortunately his plans go astray.

> When at last, wretched journey!
> All did sleep. save her and me,
> I to reach the lady's bed
> Most skilfully attempted.
> But I fell, noised it abroad,
> Tumbled brutally forward.

It's easier to be clumsy,
Rising from such grief, than spry!
Nor was my leap unhurtful:
On a stupid and loud stool,
Ostler's work, to the chagrin
Of my leg, I barked my shin;
Came up, a sorry story,
And struck – may Welshmen love me!
Too great desire is evil,
Every step unlucky still! –
By blows in mad bout betrayed,
On a table-top my forehead,
Where, all the time, a pitcher
And a loud brass cauldron were.
Collapse of that stout table –
Two trestles downed – stools as well!
Cry that the cauldron uttered
Behind me, for miles was heard;
Pitcher shouted my folly,
And the dogs barked around me.
In a foul bed, at the wall,
Bothered for their packs, and fearful,
Three English lay in panic –
Hickin and Jenkin and Jack.
The young one spluttered a curse
And hissed forth to the others:
'There's a Welshman on the prowl!'
– O hot ferment of betrayal –
'He'll rob us, if we let him!
Look out you're not a victim!'

The ostler roused all the rest –
My plight was of the direst!
All round me they were angry
And searched for me all round me.
I stood, in the foul havoc
Of rage, silent in the dark;
Prayed, in no reckless fashion,
Hiding like a frightened man:
And such power has prayer for us,
Such is the true grace of Jesus,

> I found my own bed safe and sure
> Though without sleep or treasure,
> Thank the Saints, freed of distress.
> I ask now God's forgiveness.[3]

Many writers have been brought to a pause by these last lines. How are we to take them? Serious, sincere, ironical, blasphemous? On the last line of all, Tony Conran comments, 'It leaves us gasping at his audacity', and he goes on to ask

> Is it really possible that Dafydd was the faithful child of Mother Church that his editor makes him out to be? Perhaps it is. One is always being surprised by the blasphemies of the faithful. But with this sort of irony, in the balance, I would not like to bet too heavily on the angelic leanings of Dafydd ap Gwilym.[4]

We turn now to two poems of a very different kind, poems which in their own way are as typical, or even more typical of Dafydd's work than 'Trouble at the Tavern'. They will provide us with something of the context in which the sharpness of this irony is to be set, and may remind us of themes in the poetry of praise with which we are already coming to be familiar.

Here then are two of the finest of Dafydd's poems about birds. The first is 'The Thrush'.

> Music of a thrush, clearbright
> Lovable language of light,
> Heard I under a birchtree
> Yesterday, all grace and glee –
> Was ever so sweet a thing
> Fine-plaited as his whistling?
>
> Matins, he reads the lesson,
> A chasuble of plumage on.
> His cry from a grove, his brightshout
> Over countrysides rings out,
> Hill prophet, maker of moods,
> Passion's bright bard of glenwoods.
> Every voice of the brookside

Sings he, in his darling pride,
Every sweet-metred love-ode,
Every song and organ mode,
Competing for a truelove,
Every catch for woman's love.
Preacher and reader of lore,
Sweet and clear, inspired rapture,
Bard of Ovid's faultless rhyme,
Chief prelate mild of Springtime.

From his birch, where lovers throng,
Author of the wood's birdsong,
Merrily the glade re-echoes –
Rhymes and metres of love he knows.
He on hazel sings so well
Through cloistered trees (winged angel)
Hardly a bird of Eden
Had by rote remembered then
How to recite what headlong
Passion made him do with song.[5]

As Tony Conran points out this is a poem built around two basic images, 'bright light and formal language'. It is the clear sharp sunlight of early May when the warmth of the sun can be tempered by a cold wind, giving a wonderful and uncommon brightness to our usually misty climate. It is the moment when the leaves of the trees are fully out but still retain a particular freshness in their green. In the clarity of the air the intricacy of the bird song is heard all the more distinctly.

The thrush is called here at once priest, poet and prophet. He fulfils the functions of all three. He is the celebrant of love, but he is also at the end a singer of 'an unblemished world'. He has indeed become an angel, the trees where he sings are like the cloister of a church; even the birds of Eden, in the unfallen world, would hardly have been able to equal the passion and profusion of his song.

In the last fourteen lines we have a magnificent example of the capacity of the Welsh poet to pack into a brief space a whole world of allusion. There is as we have seen a reference to the world before

the fall of the Genesis story. But there is also a hint of the
enchanted birds, who in Celtic mythology, sing in the islands of
the blessed, the birds of Rhiannon. The two themes had twined
themselves together in medieval Celtic legend and mythology. In
the Voyage of St Brendan, for instance, we read of islands where
paradisal birds sing the praises of God. But it is not only the pre-
Christian Celtic world which is evoked here. The thrush is also a
bard of Ovid's school. The whole world of classical love poetry,
Latin and Greek, is summoned to be present. Here the writer
gathers up in his conclusion an original and, I would maintain,
profoundly Christian celebration of the beauty of the world when
seen as God's creation.

The splendour of this poem can be more than matched by
another, 'The Skylark'.

Triumphant hours are the lark's
who circles skywards from his home each day:
world's early riser, with bubbling golden song,
towards the firmament, guardian of April's gate.

Gracious of voice, disposing harmonies,
sweet is your labour on a joyful course,
making a poem above the hazel grove
with the gentle feat of your grey wings.
You have a mind to preach
(dear office) and with language excellent,
a powerful song that springs from the source of faith
deep-seated privileges before the Lord.
Upwards you fly, with Cai's own attribute,
and upwards as you go you sing each song
a splendid charm near to the rampart of the stars,
a long-revolving journey to the heights.
Your feat is now accomplished, you have climbed high
        enough,
you have indeed attained to your reward.

Let each fortunate creature praise
his Maker, the immaculate pure Ruler,
let him praise God, as was decreed,
a thousand hear it. He should be praised, do not desist.

Author of the ways of love, where are you?
with dear sweet voice, dressed in grey-brown,
pure and delightful is your song,
brown songster, one inspired,
a *cantor* from the chapel of the Lord
skilled are you, and your augury is good.
Completely privileged, with well-proportioned song,
your full head-dress is a crest of grey.
Make for the familiar firmament,
song-bearing, to that wild untrodden land.

Man sees you up aloft
in truth, when day is at its height;
when you may come (thus) to worship,
this gift God One and Three has given you:
no branch of tree high up above the world
sustains you – you have (your own) speech –
but the grace of the just Father
His abundant miracles and His design.[6]

Here the image is one of ascent, and constant circling in ascent.
We might think in musical terms of the constant repetitions in
Vaughan Williams's 'The Lark Ascending'. Here again the bird is
both preacher and priest. He proclaims God's glory and calls on
all creation to unite in his praises. There is throughout the poetry
of the medieval west, whether in France, England or Wales, a
wonderful clarity of vision, a sharpness of sensuous response to
primary colours and living things. It is as if people were seeing and
saying things for the first time. Dafydd has this same quality. The
Welsh language is rich in synonyms for beauty, clarity, shining,
radiance. The whole world is full of that light, that brightness.
Here above all it is the thought of prayer which is dominant. The
bird rises towards God, penetrates into the divine world, held up
by no earthly support. It is God himself whose grace sustains him
in his song. For prayer itself is in the end God's work and not ours.
It is he who opens our lips so that our mouth may proclaim his
praise. How far Dafydd was conscious that the skylark here has
become an image of the man and woman at prayer, it is difficult to
say. He lived in a world in which the public practice of prayer was

much more in evidence than it is today, and in which the
parallels between birds and animals on the one side and human
beings on the other were affirmed in many kinds of ways. But
as T. S. Eliot pointed out a true poet is always glad to find
that his work means more than its maker knew it did, that it
contains levels of significance of which he was not consciously
aware.

Now it is not to be supposed that Dafydd was alone in seeing the
lark ascending as an image of man at prayer. In some ways it was
almost a commonplace of medieval writing. We may turn for an
example to the lines of an English fourteenth-century poet, John
Gower.

> Dieu la devocioun rejette
> Du prestre, qant il huy tresjette
> Ses heures tanq'en autre jour:
> Car qui l'en doit sanz nul destour
> Loenge rendre au creatour
> Essample avons de l'alouette
> Qui bien matin de tour en tour
> Monte, et du Dieu volant en tour
> Les laudes chante en sa gorgette.[7]

(God rejects the prayers of the priest, when he puts off saying
his office for another day. And that he ought to praise his
creator without delay take the example of the lark which early
in the morning rises up constantly turning, and flying around
God sings his praises in his throat.)

But to return to the point which was made before; in Dafydd
the birds are never simply personifications of some human trait.
To quote Chotzen again, 'Personification is always counter-
balanced by close observation of each bird's true individual
characteristics.' And while on the one side there is this close,
sensuous realization of the embodied reality of the creature being
described, there is at the same time the heightened sense of the
mystery of God, of some transcendent realm made present in its
being. The whole creation is for a moment seen transfigured. All
things are renewed in their original clarity.

Perhaps in poems such as these we have an indication of the way in which the irony and satire of a work like 'Trouble at the Tavern' may be incorporated into a total vision of the world in which, in the end, praise prevails. Without ignoring or denying the ambiguities and dissonances which are present in Dafydd's work, dissonances which respond only too well to our actual experience of life, it becomes possible to see them as themselves affirmative, an affirmation of what is there, signs of the poet's honesty and attentiveness to the world around him. Just as the medieval cathedral incorporated its gargoyles and its monsters into a building which is in the end an immense affirmation of praise and worship, so too the medieval poet did not fail to bring the grotesque and the tragic into the presence of God, allowing it too in the end to be brought to reconciliation in him.

II

In our consideration of Dafydd ap Gwilym we have been endeavouring to penetrate back into the Middle Ages, and moreover into the Middle Ages of a Celtic world which is unfamiliar to us. We come now to a period closer to our own, to times which may seem more accessible. The age of the Renaissance and the Reformation was the age of the printed book, of the great discoveries of the world beyond Europe. It was a time when the old unities and certainties of the pre-Reformation world were fractured for ever. How much, if anything, of that unity of vision which brought together God, man and creation into a single focus would be able to survive into this new and rapidly changing society?

We shall begin with Edmwnd Prys (1543/4–1623), a notable representative both of the Renaissance and Reformation. He was a man of classical learning, a product of Elizabethan Cambridge where he stayed for fifteen years; he was also a man of the Reformation in its earliest Anglican form, Archdeacon of Merioneth in the church of Elizabeth and James I. His metrical version of the Psalms of David provided the Welsh with their first vernacular hymn-book. As in the case of other representative figures of the church of his time, Lancelot Andrewes or Richard

Hooker for instance, he combines in himself elements of Reformation, Renaissance and pre-Reformation Christendom in a
remarkable way. He is a man of the new world, that is true. But he
has not altogether abandoned the old. When he sings in praise of
our redemption in his great ode on that subject, he devotes the
first half of his poem to the praise of Mary, in a long meditation on
the Lucan narrative of the annunciation. When he comes as an
old man to write an elegy on two of his contemporaries, Welsh
bishops of the period, one of them his diocesan at Bangor, he finds
it natural to begin his poem with a passage describing the
friendship of St Gregory Nazianzen and St Basil in their student
days in Athens. His own friends who had gone out from the
university into the world of the church, reminded him of the two
great Greek theologians. They too had gone on to serve the
church in the episcopal ministry.

He does all this in Welsh, because he combines with his other
qualities, that of a man devoted to the literary tradition of his
people. Not that he is uncritical of the bardic tradition as he sees it
in his own day. Quite the reverse; it seems to him increasingly
fossilized, unwilling to respond to the challenges which the new
learning provided. The conservatism of his contemporaries
appalled him. He longs for them to be more adventurous, to take
in new subjects, to take in new metres. He himself does both these
things. Football and tobacco first appear in Welsh writing in his
verses. He takes the traditional form of a poem making a request,
and uses it to ask a neighbour for the loan of a gun to protect
himself in the year of the Spanish Armada.[8]

We do not know why Edmwnd Prys did not stay in England
and make his career there. Many Welshmen in his time did so. We
do not even know why he did not stay in Ludlow, the seat of the
Tudor administration of a large part of Wales, when he had the
chance to be there. All we know is that he chose to return to
Maentwrog, to a steeply wooded valley in an extremely Welsh
part of north Wales, to a little church dedicated to a sixth-century
Celtic saint, with a pre-Christian standing stone placed beside its
porch. There he returned in 1578, and there he remained until the
time of his death, forty-five years later. He was living at the heart
of the Celtic world, a world full of the language, the literature and

the legends of his people. He himself had before his death become part of that legend. There are stories of him which might fit a Celtic wizard. There in that remote place he saw and praised the beauty of God shining out in all the beauty of the moment when spring passes into summer.

We must not make him more Celtic than he was. The poem which he wrote in praise of May-time is, as regards its style and structure, a complete innovation in the Welsh tradition. It was written to be sung to an English tune, and it has much of the form and style of an Italian madrigal of the time. Purposely and deliberately Prys adopted new fashions and new approaches to show that the Welsh language need not be weighed down and imprisoned by the achievements of its past. But the content of the poem reveals what we have already seen in the work of Dafydd, a delight in nature and in human life as ways in which God's goodness makes itself known to us. It is a poem of delight in May of a kind which we do not usually associate with an Elizabethan archdeacon.

The poem seems to hover between a description of the bird song in the newly leaved trees and a description of the songs sung in the house to celebrate the beauty of the girls of Gwynedd. Its stanzas are not always easy to interpret since they contain references to the technical terms of medieval Welsh singing and harp-playing, a musical tradition which was lost in the seventeenth century. Despite the problems over details, the general impression is clear in the dexterity of Gwyn Williams's translation.[9]

> A shout came from the loquacious ones
> whom we heard yesterday under green trees,
>   holy and church-like place,
> three lives to those gentle poets
> grove linnet, innocent nightingale,
>   pensive and paradisal,
> sweet thrush of pure oration,
> the blackbird greater in desire
> and the lascivious siskin
> who net the song of the lark . . .

When writing a poem of such metrical ingenuity, the choice of words is sometimes dictated by purely metrical criteria. But the adjectives in line three which refer to the trees, and the adjectives in line six which refer to the birds are not there just by chance. In line three we have *glwysaidd* and *eglwysaidd*, and in line six *dwysaidd* and *paradwysaidd*. In each case the first descriptive adjective *glwys* which means pleasant or beautiful, and *dwys* which means deep or intense, is coupled with a second which underlines the unity of the natural scene with the world of Eden and the world of redemption. Sacred and secular are brought together into one; there is no great gulf between them.

> A near-by grove with notes increasing,
> an April grove and primrose-full,
>   place of fine songs and daisies;
> a dale full of the spring clover
> and the green clothes of true delight
>   filling with happiness,
> with flowers on the thorn points,
> the slim birch and the fresh leaves;
> fair is the fountain, sweet the spot,
> from under the boughs there springs
>   the clear water
>   the fresh waters;
>   fair, fortunate place,
>   a place to sleep
>   a place to learn
>   all knots of descanting.

The poem, itself a text to be sung, continues with its musical references, associating human voices with the voices of nature, celebrating

> each bird in its own voice
> each tree in bright green tunic,
> each plant in its own virtue
> each bird with a poet's lips.

In the final stanza of the poem we are able to see signs of a controversy about the way of observing Sunday which was already in Elizabeth's reign dividing the stricter Puritans from more traditional churchmen. This conflict became particularly sharp in the seventeenth century, in the period before the Civil War. It is no surprise to find Prys here underlining the appropriateness of Sunday for innocent enjoyment. The sabbath, he holds, is made for man, not man for the sabbath. What is more striking is the generally affirmative nature of these lines, not always paralleled in his other poems, which sometimes take a much darker view of the human condition. Here we have a vision of the divine blessing resting on the world of nature and on the whole human enterprise 'as long as there's no sin'. It is a way of seeing the eternal world mirrored in the world of time, which brings us close to the vision of Dafydd ap Gwilym at its most positive.

> Delight is good for all mankind
> and merriment for maidens,
>   Sunday is good for men;
> this is fair and not odious for age
> fair, not unpleasant, for youth
>   the green and flowering meadows
> planned fair by the true God Father,
> his gift and notable grace.
> Each voice is fair, every turn,
> as long as there's no sin.
>   On earth
>   how gentle;
>   early on the wheat
>   and on the grove;
>   how mild the land
> where the great blessing's given!

III

If in Edmwnd Prys the unified vision of the Middle Ages seems to cross the division made by Reformation and Renaissance, how will it be after another two centuries, which have seen the virtual disappearance of the Welsh bardic schools along with the Welsh-speaking aristocracy which sustained them? Can the tradition continue in such unpropitious times? Can it survive into the age of Newton and Locke?

To respond to these questions we shall turn to the writings of one who has a no less important place in the religious history of Wales than Edmwnd Prys, perhaps the most learned of the early leaders of Welsh Calvinistic Methodism, Thomas Jones of Denbigh, (1756–1820). Here again we have a scholar, a preacher and a poet. But unlike Edmwnd Prys, Thomas Jones was not the product of any university. As a young man he refused his father's offer of a place at Oxford or Cambridge, preferring the fellowship of the Methodists at Caerwys, mostly farm-hands, small shop-keepers and artisans, to the comforts of an eighteenth-century college. Thomas Jones became a very learned man, but he was self-taught. He became known as a great controversialist, defending a moderate Calvinist position against the Arminianism of the followers of Wesley on the one side, and the hyper-Calvinism of John Elias and his friends on the other. The details of these arguments need not concern us here. Thomas Jones was able, out of his knowledge of the history of Christian thought, to approach them with a balance and perspective unusual in his time. He was evidently a man of large and deeply pondered views.

He was also a person whose life had not been particularly easy. He knew not only ill health, but also times of inward darkness and depression. Reading his sermons and meditations one has the impression of a man who had learnt compassion through the things he had undergone. But if he knew the experience of the absence of God, and had had to walk in darkness, it is no less evident that he had entered deeply into the experience of the divine light. He is a writer to whom it is not inappropriate to apply the word 'mystical', so surely does he speak of the mystery of our unity with God in Christ through the coming of the Holy Spirit. He tells us of our call to become partakers of all the fullness of God, not only of the promises of God but also of the properties of God, not only of what God has but also of what God is, in a way which reveals the presence of a man who had seen far into the secrets of the divine wisdom. His writings provide us with a vital clue to understanding some of the deepest elements in the vision of Ann Griffiths.

Scarcely less surprising is a meditation of his on the nature of creation, with its suggestion of a gradual transition from the world of time and space into the world of God's eternity, and its strong affirmation of the presence of God's wisdom in and through the whole material world. He writes,

> 'In this sublime and splendid edifice', he writes 'I can see three levels of the nobility of being; the first encompasses the birds, the mists and the winds; the second is for the stars; and the third is reserved for the saints and the angels. The first is a court which is open to all; the second is like a temple in which the candles of heaven burn unceasingly; and the third is reserved to the saints and the angels . . . We experience the first, perceive the second, and believe concerning the third. But in the third level you, O eternal Trinity, find joy in yourself, and you are the bliss of the spirits you have glorified. It is the manifestation of your glory which makes heaven what it is. This is the privilege of your children; by perceiving you here through faith they are beginning that perfect heaven, which they will enjoy perfectly when they have perfect vision of you.'[10]

It is very important to notice that for him already here and now we begin through faith to perceive the glory which we shall behold in its perfection hereafter. There is a way which leads us up through the lower levels of being, through the outer courts of the temple, into the very presence of God. We see this same scheme worked out in one of Thomas Jones's most notable poems for, like Edmwnd Prys, Thomas Jones was a fine poet as well as a scholar and a divine.

But whereas Prys when he wrote of springtime chose to do so in a fashionable Italian Renaissance metre, Thomas Jones two centuries later preferred the style and manner of Dafydd ap Gwilym, consciously following the model of the great fourteenth-century poet whose works had been printed for the first time a few years before he wrote his poem to a song thrush in 1793. In itself it is surprising enough that a late eighteenth-century Calvinist theologian and preacher should write a long and accomplished poem in the style of a fourteenth-century love poet. What is still more striking is the content of the poem. Here we have a prime example of the living continuity of Welsh tradition, both in form

and content. It is scarcely possible to think of a poet in any of the
other major European languages at this period, who would have
had this kind of access to the vision and the resources of the
Middle Ages.[11]

Thomas Jones's poem is well over two hundred lines long.
The earlier sections speak of the thrush with that kind of
delighted detail of observation of its flight and its song
which we have already seen in Dafydd. This is a real thrush
as the poet has seen him, as he rests at his home after a
period of illness. It is only towards the end that he begins
directly to reflect on the meaning of the bird and its song in
relation to his faith in the God revealed in Jesus Christ. Then,
as we shall see, he does it in ways which are already familiar
to us.

> Frail bird of taught loveliness
> You enrich and you astound us.
> We wonder long at your song,
> Your artistry and your voice.
> In you I see, I believe,
> A splendid and unique work of God,
> He is glorious and glorified
> Showing his virtue in the smallest creature.
> How many bright wonders (clear note of loveliness)
> Does this world contain?
> How many parts, how many mirrors of his splendid work
> Offer themselves a hundred times to our gaze?
> For the book of his art is a speaking light
> Of lines abundantly full,
> And every day one chapter after another
> Comes among us to teach us of him.
>
> The smallest part of the work of his most lovely hand
> Becomes our teacher, lordly and true.
> A winged and lively bird,
> Who gives an impromptu sermon
> Who teaches us much
> Of our Lord, who is Master,
> Of his power and his wealth
> And of his wisdom great and true

If our Lord is great, and great is his praise
From just this one small part of earth
Then what of the image of his greatness
Which springs from his work in its fullness?
Through the image of the ascending steps
Of that gracious work, which he has made
(Below and above the firmament the number of his
Marvels is without number)
What of the greatness
Which is that pure loveliness
Of our God himself?[12]

So in his poem Thomas Jones sees the world as a book in which
God writes for our instruction, sees the thrush as our teacher who
tells us of the greatness and beauty of the Lord. He ascends from
his loving meditation on this one fragile creature, which in itself is
a mirror of the eternal loveliness of God, to a consideration of the
totality of God's work, in which his glory is to be seen more fully
and from there to the contemplation of the divine glory in itself.
One could not wish for a fuller or more exact illustration of the
way in which the specifically Celtic vision of the relationship
between God and his creation, a vision which has deep roots
within the biblical tradition, was alive at the turn of the
eighteenth century, present at the heart of early nineteenth-
century Methodism in Wales.

The Gift of Sight: twentieth-century transformations

In the two previous chapters we have looked very briefly at the development of the praise tradition in Welsh poetry over a period of a thousand years. Our treatment of the subject has necessarily been rapid and highly selective. In this and the following chapter we shall be looking at the same theme in terms of the twentieth century. Here again we shall have to be very selective, for one of the outstanding facts about the Welsh tradition is the extraordinary richness of the last ninety years. At a time when the proportion of Welsh-speakers has been constantly falling, so that it now stands at less than twenty per cent of the whole population, there has been a flowering of poetic genius unequalled since the golden age of the fourteenth and fifteenth centuries. A recently published anthology of twentieth-century verse runs to almost 700 pages.[1] The outer loss has gone along with an inner gain, which no statistician could have foreseen.

Even more remarkable is the fact that in the last fifty years, to be precise since around 1936, a large part of this poetic production has been the work of poets of deeply Christian convictions. At a time when all the churches at the public and institutional level have been declining in influence and numbers, a decline which has been particularly sharp in some areas of Welsh Nonconformity, there has been a reaffirmation of Christian vision which is admirable and wholly unexpected.

This renewal of Christian vision is not the work of any one group or school of writers. One of the most striking facts about the poets of the last half century is their diversity, both as writers and as men. This diversity extends to the question of their denominational allegiance. One thing which they had in common is a

tendency to move from one tradition to another as if seeking a
fuller realization of the breadth and length of the Christian
mystery than is easily to be found in any one of our denominations
as currently existing. Saunders Lewis (1893–1985), for instance,
beginning as a Calvinistic Methodist became a Roman Catholic,
and in the latter years of his life went out of his way to affirm
everything that was common to the tradition in which he was
brought up and the tradition which he entered. Waldo Williams
was brought up as a Baptist. In mature life he became a Quaker,
and in his latter days he had many contacts with Roman
Catholics and acknowledged the influence of the Russian Orthodox thinker, Nicholas Berdyaev. Gwenallt (1899–1968) also came
from a Calvinistic Methodist background and became an
Anglican of distinctly Catholic flavour. Towards the end of his
life, when faced with the unacceptable Englishness of some of the
members of the Anglican hierarchy, he returned to the church of
his baptism, while never repudiating his Catholic convictions.
Euros Bowen (1904–89) was, by family background a Congregationalist, but in his student years he became an Anglican and
was ordained to the priesthood in the Church in Wales. He alone
of the four mentioned was ordained. The others were all teachers
either in school or in university. What is striking about them all,
and about many of their younger contemporaries, whose work I
shall cite, is that despite great differences of literary style and
attitude, despite their different histories of church belonging,
when they write poetry they recognizably belong to the same
overall tradition, a tradition which sees the whole world as
sacramental, which affirms the communion of saints across the
barrier of death, which wishes above all to see God in and through
his creation and not in opposition to it.

Of course they are men of the twentieth century. This means
that they are conscious as regards their Christian faith that it
cannot be untroubled and unquestioned. All are aware of the
weight of disbelief and despair which hangs over our century. But
this also means that as writers in Welsh they are inheritors of the
revival of Welsh learning and scholarship which began in the last
years of the nineteenth century in connection with the development of Welsh studies in the newly founded colleges of the

University of Wales. This means that they have a conscious grasp
of the earlier periods of their own tradition, and of its links with
the tradition of the Celtic world as a whole, which their
predecessors in the eighteenth and nineteenth centuries did not
have. All, in their own way, affirm the unity and continuity of this
Welsh tradition. Euros, for example, does it in a remarkable long
poem called 'Golau' (Light), which traces its growth through the
many and violent vicissitudes of Welsh history. Gwenallt and
Waldo do it in poems which speak explicitly about the communion of saints. Saunders Lewis makes this affirmation not only
in his poetry but in the great and highly impressive body of his
literary critical and historical work, work in which he surveys the
whole Welsh tradition and shows its underlying themes and
motives with an unusual fusion of exact scholarship and sympathetic imagination.

I am impelled to say, of these writers, though the judgement is
almost bound to be misunderstood, that *when they write as poets* they
write as Catholics. By which I do not mean that they write with
any anti-Protestant bias or animus, but that they write af-
firmatively as men who want to assert the fullness and balance of
the Christian faith, who want to recognize and live by the
wholeness of the tradition, and who have a vision of its unity and
coherence greater than that which is realized at the canonical
level by any of our churches at the present time. This is a
Catholicism both of east and west alike, which is aware of the
strange and elusive affinities between Celtic Christianity and the
eastern Christian world. It is a Catholicism which does not reject
the affirmations of the Renaissance or the convictions of the
Reformation, but which seeks to understand how to make them its
own. In their poetry at least – I do not speak here of their prose
writing – there is nothing sectarian or polemical in a divisive
sense. What there is, is a triumphant affirmation of faith against
the unbelief and distrust of our age, of hope against our tendencies
to an easy despair, and of love for God and his creation against all
our temptations to shut ourselves up in a narcissistic cocoon. All of
them are calling us to look out and see the world which is around
us, to see that it is the world in which God himself has placed us,
and is actively at work.

I

One of the words in Welsh which is difficult, if not impossible, to translate into English is *synhwyrus*. It is an adjective which means 'perceived by the senses'. It is not *sensitive*, for that has a gentle almost feeble sound to it in English, and *synhwyrus* is strong and active. It is not *sensuous* for that in modern English has too specialized a meaning, it is too much a matter of silks and satins and languors. It might in the past have been translated by *sensible*; but that is no longer possible since at least in common usage the word has connotations of caution and prudence from which the senses are virtually excluded. But the Welsh poets of the twentieth century again and again are calling us to open our eyes to see and our ears to hear. They are calling on us to perceive the world in which we live and to perceive God in it. Gwenallt begins one of his finest sonnets, with the affirmation 'God has not forbidden us to love the world' and he ends it by speaking of that day of resurrection when the body will be restored to us, so that we may *synhwyruso gogoniannau Duw*, 'perceive the glories of God with all our senses'. To *sniff* them would be one possible translation of the line.[2]

Of course in calling us to see things, and declaring what they themselves see, the poets of our own time are fulfilling the oldest of all the bardic functions, that of sight. The bards were seers, men of vision, who declared what they saw, who sang the glory of God perceived in all his doings.

I caught a glimpse of Your court from a ridge in Plynlimon;
I saw its border from a plain in Anglesey.
And the wounded walls of autumn were a mark of its glory,
And the boldness of spring, like one of heaven's out-
    buildings.
A court of judgment, a king's court. My head was wide-open
In wonder that it was, and that it was so comely,
When You called out, on the part of Your estate
That is east of Defynnog: 'Be a poet
For me.' For You, Lord! For You, Arbiter of Living!
'For me.' Your graces run the breadth of the world;
You stand at the table sharing mysterious drinks,

A king of generous gifts. You leave Your trace
In a child, a word and a church, in a view,
And in every season, Lord, You are good.
Already in December the breeze is budding
In the lowest hour: You express in every region
Your expectation. Everything is Your estate,
And in every place one finds food. For in the worst of the cold
Your wound is Your diadem . . . the Lord who bends his
      knee . . .
(Giving to all in need from Your own possessions)
And my young patron who turns Your wanting to wine.[3]

The poem 'Bardd Llys' (Court Poet) is the work of Bobi Jones,
one of the most prolific of contemporary Welsh writers, scholar,
poet and man of faith; a passionate, conservative Evangelical by
religious persuasion. It is a poem which speaks for itself of the
poet's sense of calling, the constraint to respond, the constraint to
give utterance to the praise which all things long to present before
their Lord. It is not only in the exuberance of springtime and the
splendours of autumn that God is to be perceived. In the darkness
and cold of December, in the lowest hour of human loss and
despondency, in the moment of God's apparent absence, there he
is most intimately present. It is in the cross that the heights and
depths of God's glory are revealed. The wounds of the Lord
become worships, as Julian of Norwich declares. In accepting our
poverty into himself, he gives to all in need from the infinite riches
of his possessions.

We turn to another poem, 'Y Berth' (The Bush) which even
more strongly represents the original bardic vocation to see and to
sing.

> I celebrate a bush that belongs
> To the ancient line of sunshine and woods
>
> In the pure earth she puts forth her roots,
> And like one whose hand holds her in place
> She is firm, a power rises,
> A secret from the soil to enlighten the wood.
>
> I saw fire, – her leaves' green was
> open for its arriving;

The flames rose from the roots, creating
A great stir in the twigs and causing thereafter
Blossoming in the branches, –
Because the green growth was not consumed,
But throve, flourished in the fire;
The powers of life purified the bush
And before the wonder of blossoms,
The blossoms of fire that burgeoned
A brilliant miracle over the bush,
I marvelled, I stood amazed.
The fire freshened the land,
A fire of every growth's vitality
And a fire of vision:
It enlightened the bush, it brightened the world.

I celebrate the bush, her beauty's flame
Entices the wind, and ignites the song,
Sustains strength, enkindles night
And day an ecstatic fire;
I celebrate the bush that bonfires
Her splendour's spring
High to the sky and scatters the breeze
And brings summer's life to the face of the land.
I see her henceforth lighting my world,
And her vision's lofty crest will be
A praise to the Lord forever.

I climb through the fire undying –
Because her fire bestows her growth;
And there I gather her fruit, and her ripeness is full,
So unblemished is the bush's season –
And I will have her harvest to stave off hunger
By storing her wealth in the heart.[4]

Here the poet is another of our contemporaries, James
Nicholas, a former archdruid, and inspector of schools in north
Wales, a Baptist lay preacher, a much less prolific poet, but none
the less one at the centre of the tradition. In this poem he sees the
whole world in the bush which is alive with the flame of growth in
springtime. There is here of course an allusion to the burning bush
which Moses saw in the wilderness, the bush which burns but is

not consumed. It is instructive that in eastern Christendom especially the burning bush has been taken as a symbol of Mary, the human being who is in a special way caught up in the fire of the divine life which grows within her body. In this poem too there is a hint that the bush is a symbol of a person, for the poem has a particular dedication to the poet's wife. The fact that the word for bush in Welsh is feminine is, of course, of assistance here. But there is also a reference here to the tree which is spoken of in Celtic mythology, a tree which is half in flame and half in leaf. The world is full of the fire of the liveliness of all growth. Heaven and earth alike are full of God's glory. The poet sees this; he sings of it; he gets caught up into it. He climbs through the bush unharmed. Like the young men in the burning, fiery furnace of Nebuchadnezzar, he finds that the fire is not a fire of destruction, but of purification. He walks through the fire unharmed and discovers it to be the fire of divine love.

The moment of vision can take many forms. It need not be solitary, it can be shared, especially it can be shared by man and woman together, husband and wife seeing into the mystery of the divine life revealed in the interaction of the opposites of which our world is made up.

> As we gazed, you and I, beloved,
> at the sunshine coupling with the shallows,
> we knew that the sun and the water were
> alive.
> We were seized in the paean of revelation
> and possessed the reality of the sparkling
> yellow-white
> copulating with the lapping grey-blue.
> They were alive.
> Not the same kind of life
> as our life,
> but they were alive;
> prince and princess,
> god and goddess,
> a *yang* and *yin* in exultation.
> And yet there is no life for them
> apart from our love:

you and I
standing on the shore
and seeing and rejoicing
in the watery sparks
and the flowing rays
and sensing that some of the light
was stored in the reeds
and some of the play
settled in the rabbits' warren.
And we knew that the love
had flooded over us,
and that Dwynwen cast out all doubts
with her 'It is not loving if joy is lacking.'
These overbrimming lovers had
no being
apart from us;
the shameless conjoining could not be
unless our eyes were gazing where they were
and over the waters
beneath the purity of the sun at zenith.
Our life gave life
to the mischievous two gods,
our life that could never be
without the conjunction of sun and water.[5]

'Llanddwyn' is a wonderful poem marked by what Les Murray calls 'a strange simultaneity of stillness and racing excitement'. It is a poem which is truly dreamed and at the same time truly thought, a remarkable fusion of reason and imagination. Pennar Davies, its author, a Congregationalist minister, and former Principal of a Free Church theological college, is a striking example of the *poeta doctus*, the learned poet. Here he has drawn into his work a suggestion of the Chinese vision of the interaction of *yin* and *yang*, the opposing principles out of which our world is made, light and dark, passive and active, male and female, sun and water. He has reflected too on the relation between the inner and the outer realms, between our inner human experience and our capacity for speech on the one side, without which the elements would be dumb, their dance of interchange unobserved, and on the other, the fact that our life, our vision, our poetic utterance, are all dependent on the physical conditions which sustain our being, the interplay of fire and water without which we cannot live.

But this very twentieth-century poem is put under the patronage of St Dwynwen. The incident takes place at her shrine, Llanddwyn on the coast of Anglesey, looking across the Menai Straits to the great panorama of Snowdonia on the other side of the sea. Dwynwen is the patron saint of lovers. Her legend, which comes to us from the early centuries of the Celtic Church speaks of a woman with a vocation to the monastic life, whose renunciation of human love for the sake of divine love yet becomes fruitful and affirmative at the human level. Those who came on pilgrimage to her prayed that they might be successful in their quest of love, and that if they were not, they should be liberated from the bonds of an unrequited love. The story of Dwynwen, one of the number of legends from the Celtic period which speak of the beneficent action of women saints (we might think of Brigid in Ireland, or of Melangell in the Berwyns), gives us yet another example of the creative conjunction of apparent opposites, the call to celibacy and the call to marriage. But all this is conveyed in the poem through the evocation of a moment of shared vision, the evocation of a moment of shared joy.

II

We have moved here towards a more cosmic understanding of the consequences of the moment of vision, and nowhere in the poetry of twentieth-century Wales is this cosmic reference more perfectly expressed than in a poem by Saunders Lewis, 'A Daisy in April'.

> Yesterday I saw a daisy
> Like a shining mirror of the dawn.
> The day before I walked over it without thought.
> Yesterday I saw. I well know
> The energy and the passion of spring and its zest,
> Creating the crystalline shilling,
> The longing of the art of the heath,
> The ruby and the gem in the marsh.
> The field where the April cuckoo sang
> Has become the milky way:

The firmament turned upside down
Millions of the suns in the heavens
Are placed beneath my feet,
To gild the grass of this grey earth.
Orion on the hillsides
Arcturus and Sirius are
Sparks of the fire of God's living coals;
Stars like seraphim
In the splendid azure sky.
Yesterday, I saw a daisy.[6]

The number of poems which Saunders Lewis published was relatively small. He was perhaps too exacting a critic of himself to allow much past the censor. As a consequence all that is in the single volume of his work has a particular excellence. This deceptively simple poem turns out to be a work of unlooked-for depth and complexity.

The first thing to be observed is that the Welsh term for 'daisy' is *llygad y dydd*, 'eye of the day'. The term is first recorded in Welsh in the fourteenth century, at a time when the English word was still pronounced 'day's-eye', making the equivalence between them obvious. Then we notice that this poem, more perhaps than any of the others which we have looked at, turns entirely on the act of seeing. The poet tells us that he has come to see what before he did not see. Yesterday, he saw a daisy, he noticed the smallest, the commonest, the least regarded of all wild flowers; or is it simply a weed? He saw it suddenly as a brightly shining mirror in which the dawn itself was reflected. He looked into the little flower and saw its great golden centre. Suddenly he recognized there an image of the sun, the eye of the day in the heavens. As the sun rises, so the flower opens itself and reveals the hidden sun at its heart. The little sun in the daisy looks back to the great sun seen in the sky. The great is reflected in the little; the little holds within itself an image of the great. And both things, the plant under our feet and the star in the sky above are themselves images, mirrors which reflect something of the brightness of the one who is called the sun of righteousness, the eye of the eternal day.

In the tiny plant all the passionate energy of the spring is present. Indeed we may rightly see all the longing which goes into our art in the creation of this crystal shilling. For if humankind is made in God's image and likeness, and if that image is most intensely realized in the act of artistic creation, then we may surely suppose that in the Creator himself there must be something which corresponds to the joy, the ecstasy of the human act of creation. God too comes out of himself, puts himself into the work of his hands, becomes embodied in some measure in the stuff of his creation. And like a human poem, what is made by God is at once 'finite yet inexhaustible'. Each flower has its own perfection, each one is different. Each one is a sun. So a million suns are scattered across the field before us. We find the Milky Way beneath our feet, adorning the grass of this grey world. Orion, Arcturus, Sirius, the ancient names for the stars, heavy with the wealth of associations, are beneath us as well as above. In all we can see the splendour of God in the splendour of his creative wisdom, for the Word of God who is God wills in all things and at all times to work the mystery of his embodiment.

The poem shows us something of the interrelatedness of the different levels of being, and their varied reflection of the divine glory. In particular it shows us something of the special worth, the special significance of what is small, fragile, commonplace and disregarded. It is in the daisy, of all things, that we see the sun. We see here that all things are knit together in harmony and all are dependent on one another. The intuitive vision of the poet is confirmed in a different level of discourse by the analytical investigation of the ecologist, who demonstrates the interaction of the smallest and apparently least important elements in the environment with those whose value is obvious and accepted. And at yet another level this vision corresponds to the teaching and insight of the moralist, the one who seeks to discern the ways in which all human beings should relate to and interact with one another. Here is the meaning of certain deeds and certain sayings of Jesus, which assert the worth of children, the birds of the air, the flowers of the field. It is in the smallest and the least regarded that God lets himself be known and loved.

As we have seen already Thomas Jones of Denbigh worked this out in one way. Saunders Lewis has expressed it in another. Both are following the Gospel precept to open our ears to hear and our eyes to see the infinite, unexplored mystery hidden in what is most ordinary and despised. He who is above all thought and all imagining makes himself known and loved by the senses, becomes 'that which we have seen and heard, and our hands have handled, the Word of Life'. The faith that God wills to be embodied in all things, and that in that sense his action is universal, does not exclude or replace faith in the central and unique mystery of the one Incarnation. Rather it is there in the focal place of his incarnate presence in Nazareth and Jerusalem that we see the possibility of his embodiment in all things.

In exactly the same way, to recognize the potentially sacramental nature of all things in no sense takes away from the necessity for the particular presence to be found in the one great sacrament of God's love. The sacramental presence of Christ in the Eucharistic elements is to be seen in relation to his universal presence in the world which he has made and redeemed. There are of course many different modes of presence, that is true. Theology has been quite right in making that clear. There is nothing to be gained from confusion and lack of clarity. But they are all of them modes of one and the same presence. It is the same Word of God who is present in a multitude of ways, and perhaps in a world like ours which for the most part feels itself to be deprived of the presence of God, cut off from all actual contact with him, it is more important to stress what is common to all these instances of divine presence than to underline what distinguishes them. It is the one Word of God who is at work in all things.

III

Here again it is interesting to notice how the interpenetration of grace and nature has found new expression in the twentieth century in Wales in a series of poems which see the interrelatedness of the sacrament of the Lord's Supper first with all shared meals, then with the whole creation.

On the first point, we may listen to Bobi Jones again, in the poem 'Having our Tea', which was written when his first child was about two years old.

There's something religious in the way we sit
At the tea table, a tidy family of three.
You, my love, slicing the bread and butter and she,
The red-cheeked tot a smear of blackberry jam, and me.
Apart from the marvellous doting
Of a world's interchange with each other . . . there's tea.
Stupid, they say, to think of the thing as an ordinance.
And yet all the elements are found to change in our hands.
Because we sit and share them with each other
There's a miracle. There's a binding of unmerited graces
By the cheese, and through the apples and the milk
A new creation of life is established, a true presence.
And talking to each other, breaking words over food
Is somehow different from customary chatting.
I know perfectly well that the generations must,
Of necessity, have performed this petty action.
And surely their pattern has long since burrowed
As part of our consciousness. Then too, back beyond the epochs
Is depending, turning back to the fountainhead,
And listening on the connecting wires to a Voice
That is at the same time food – he expresses
Himself here from the beginning. All would acknowledge
That the food itself is a pleasure:
The spirit grows stronger too in its wake.
Still tea is not worship . . . But it overcomes
Things so the spirit may happily hop
In our hearts. Assimilating heaven's carol
Into our constitutions, we are a choir, our throats
Blending calories and words together in the presence
Of the unseen Conductor who laid the table.[7]

Once we have seen how every meal is in some way a miracle, we
shall be a little less anxious about recognizing the miraculous
element in the particular meal which the Lord has given us in
memory of himself. If at tea time the things which are shared are
found to change in our hands, how much more must it be so at the
Lord's Table. Of course the poet is far too exact a theologian to
confuse the family tea with the Lord's Supper itself. It is not
strictly speaking worship, what in another tradition might be
termed a liturgy. Still there is here as in the liturgy a true presence

of the Lord in our midst, and a creation of new life. The Spirit is present, overcoming the things which divide us and weigh us down, making the new wine of the Kingdom present for us, with all its joy, yes even through the milk and the biscuits and the children's tea.

It is a poem which might be thought to be almost too comfortably domestic, if it did not have within it the suggestion of the untold generations of human beings for whom the practice of eating and drinking together has established one of the most basic patterns of human society. Here, in the middle of the poem, unimaginably long vistas open up which puzzle and attract us. We see that the ordinance is not only a type of human social life. It has a still wider, cosmic significance.

It is this aspect of the rite which is central to the last two poems which we shall consider on this theme. Both, in different ways, speak of the Eucharist as it is seen in relation to the consecration of the whole creation. 'Reredos' is the work of Euros Bowen, himself a priest, and it speaks of a celebration of the Eucharist taking place in the chapel of a house in Anglesey, a chapel which had a glass window behind the altar, looking out across the Menai Strait, into the mountains of Snowdonia. It happens that the Archbishop of Wales was the celebrant on the occasion which gave rise to this vivid and compact meditation.

> The reredos was not
> an ecclesiastical adornment
> of symbols,
> but plain glass
> with the danger
> of distracting the celebrant
> from
> the properties of the communion table,
>
> for
> in the translucence
> the green earth
> budded in the morning view,
> the river was in bloom,
> the air a joyous flight,

and the sunshine
set the clouds ablaze,

and I noticed
the priest's eyes
as it were unconsciously
placing his hand
on these gifts,
as though these
were
the bread and wine.[8]

The church's celebration is not shut in on itself, confined by a screen of 'ecclesiastical symbols', symbols which often in our western churches have become dead and purely conventional. It is open to the world, and there are dangers in the fact, dangers of distraction, dangers of confusion. Like Bobi Jones, Euros Bowen was too clear a thinker, too good a theologian – he had translated Athanasius's 'On the Incarnation' into Welsh – to be satisfied with anything vaguely sentimental in a matter of this kind. No, the gifts of nature are not precisely 'the properties of the communion table', but they are related to them, and it is this relationship which the plain glass window allows us to perceive. The consecration of the one implies the consecration of the other. The sacrifice of praise and thanksgiving which the church offers in obedience to the Lord's command has implications for the whole of human life, and ultimately for the whole creation. The bread and the wine are of the same stuff, consubstantial with the whole created order. They are at once the fruit of the earth and the work of human hands. The natural order and the human order come together in them, and together are offered to God and changed by the Spirit.

But the supreme expression of this theme in contemporary Welsh poetry is to be found in the work of Saunders Lewis. In one sense this is not surprising. Saunders Lewis explained on one occasion that it was the Mass above everything else which had brought him into communion with Rome. He found that here at the altar there was the full, complete, God-given vehicle of human adoration and praise, the presence of the one perfect sacrifice of

Christ. So as he said more than once, 'The Mass makes sense of everything'. Here heaven and earth are united, earth is redeemed and glorified. There are a number of his poems which in a variety of ways speak about the action of the Mass. This is a poem which speaks of the Mass above all in terms of praise, the praise which arises from the world of nature. It is full of reminiscences of Dafydd ap Gwilym, and his 'Mass in the Grove'. It is called 'Ascension Thursday'.

What's going on in the hills, this May morning?
Look at it all, the gold on the broom and the laburnum,
The shoulders of the thorntree bright with its surplice,
The ready emerald of grass, the quiet calves;

The chestnut trees have their candlesticks alight,
Hedgerows are kneeling, the birch is still as a nun,
The cuckoo's two notes over the hush of bright streams
And a ghost mist bending away from the mead's censer;

From the council houses men come – Oh come out before
The rabbits all scatter! With the weasel come and see
A wafer immaculate lifted from the earth
And the Father kiss the Son in the white dew.[9]

Seen from one point of view the poem is a description of that miraculous moment in the early morning in springtime in the countryside, which everything in our current urban way of life seems to conspire to keep us from experiencing. The brightness, the silence, the cuckoo's reiterated call, the mist rising up from the meadows, the animals themselves apparently in some kind of hushed expectation. But looked at again we notice that we are present in the church's liturgy, present indeed at the moment of consecration in a High Mass as celebrated in the Latin rite as it was before the liturgical changes of Vatican II. The surpliced servers kneel at the altar step, the candles burn steadily in the old-fashioned candle-stand, the smoke of the incense rises as the censer is swung, the sound of the sacring bell rings out across the silence, the celebrant lifts up the host for the adoration of the people. And the Father kisses the Son in the white dew.

For Saunders Lewis the Mass is not only the offering of sacrifice,
it is also the wedding of heaven and earth in which God and man
are united, and God's people are knit together into one. They are
united by the action of God himself, God giving himself in his
creation, to his creation, for his creation. This gift of God, which is
God, is the name of the Holy Spirit in whose power alone all the
mysteries of the church are celebrated. He is the kiss who unites
the Father and the Son. It is the expression of some of the greatest
of the church's theologians. He it is who is imaged as the dew
which descends on the earth refreshing it and making it fertile. It
is He who is invoked when the church prays that 'the continual
dew of God's blessing' may rest on all its members. So it is that in
the white dew – and in Welsh as in Breton the word *gwyn* means
holy as well as white – the offering of the Son is accepted by the
Father, and in the Son's ascension all creation is lifted up into
communion with the divine life. For Christ is one, in the words of
the Athanasian creed, 'not by conversion of the Godhead into
flesh, but by taking of the manhood into God'.

It would not be like Saunders Lewis to leave us without
unanswered questions, uncomfortable points which leave us
dissatisfied. Why are we to come 'with the weasel'? Perhaps to
remind us of the sinister, predatory side of the creation, even in
this apparently paradisal moment. At least that is possible. More
important, is there not something unpleasantly sneering in the
reference to 'the council houses' from which we are exhorted to
come out? Some have thought so. Is this a little bit of upper-
middle class, professional snobbery; a condescending reference to
lower orders who are likely to keep the coal in the bath? It can be
read in that way. But I would suggest that the phrase contains
another allusion, this time to one of Ann Griffiths's letters, for
which we know Saunders Lewis had the highest regard. In this
letter Ann declares that all Christian people are called to come out
from their own ceiled houses, in order to see the King in the
wonder and glory of the cross. Her meaning seems clearly to be
that we have to come out of the small world of our own
distractions and anxieties, ambitions and achievements, the small
world of our own opinions and ideas, in order to see beyond them,
to look towards the uncreated beauty of the divine light, which we

shall only be able to see in so far as we die to our own ideas and begin to live with the life of God. Council houses are usually rather small and uniform. They often seem to be drab and unexciting. There could hardly be an apter image for the kind of life in which people are tempted to enclose themselves, with its lazy habits of mind and feelings, a life which seems temptingly cosy and familiar, but which in the end turns our to be stifling and self-destructive.

We remarked at the beginning of this chapter that there seemed to be some ecumenical significance in the varied patterns of ecclesiastical allegiance which can be traced in the lives of the writers we have been considering. Quite specifically this would seem to be the case with the last three writers whose work has been examined. Each in his own way, from within his own community of faith, has made an affirmation about that central act of worship which all who seek to follow Jesus celebrate in obedience to his command, Do this in remembrance of me. There is tragedy and paradox in the fact that they make this affirmation from within communities which are not in canonical communion with one another. There is hope in the fact that they can together affirm so much, and that the relationships between the churches from which they come, though still wounded and uncertain, seem in the perspective of half a century to be almost miraculously in the way of healing.

Two Worlds in One: heaven on earth

The picture of the world given in the last chapter may seem excessively affirmative. Does the sun always shine in Wales? What about the dark side of human life, the experience of loss and betrayal, of pain and death? Do the poets have nothing to say about that?

As we remarked earlier, a vein of satire and mockery has been a necessary corrective in a tradition which has built itself around the act of praise. That element of satire is not lacking in the writing of the twentieth century. In some of the poems of Saunders Lewis it takes on an almost surrealist savagery of tone. It is also marked in his poetry, as well as in that of others, by the quality of anger, the anger of those who see great injustices and evils and find themselves unable to do anything, at least externally, to right them, the anger of those who long to stir their nation into action, and find themselves faced with a huge indifference and apathy.

In this respect, some of Gwenallt's poems are perhaps more typical than the writings of Saunders Lewis. David James Jones (Gwenallt) was the most openly and outspokenly religious of the poets of the mid century. His critics sometimes said that he turned his poems into sermons. This directness about Gwenallt's writing makes it in some ways unusually accessible to translation. He was born into an industrial working-class family in the south. His father was killed in a hideous industrial accident, a fall of molten metal. In his adolescence Gwenallt turned his back on the Nonconformity in which he had grown up, and became a Marxist. He was imprisoned during the First World War in Wormwood Scrubs and in Dartmoor, as a member of the ILP, refusing military service on political grounds as much as on religious ones. The experience of being in prison has been one shared by some of the greatest Welsh poets of this century, Gwenallt, Waldo and Saunders Lewis himself. Gradually Gwenallt found his way back to Christian faith, not repudiating his socialism as he did so, but integrating it into a larger and more finally satisfying vision of man and society. In the 1940s he became an Anglican, and his Anglicanism had a decidedly Catholic quality. The sacramental vision which Gwenallt expresses with remarkable power was something which he never repudiated even though in later life he returned to the Calvinistic Methodist tradition of his upbringing. He had a particularly strong sense of the communion of saints as we shall see in the poem 'Adrift'.

Let him speak for the distress of the thirties.

> Woe to us who know the words without knowing the
> Word that is there
> And sell our souls for the toffee and confetti of a fair,
> Follow after every drum and dance after every flute
> And drown the Intercession's hymn with the gabble of
> the Absolute.
>
> Men in the South of Wales without food or drink or a fag,
> The glory of their countryside under scrapheaps,
> cinders, slag,
> The canal in villages dawdling, no ford, no movement,
> no sound.
> And the big-bellied rats devouring the corpses of cat
> and hound.
>
> In our lands fortune and fate and chance are now the
> gods on top,
> And we ourselves are like moles that have been caught
> in their trap;
> Beneath the paper floors of our world is neither hell nor
> devil,
> Heaven's candles have been put out, and strangled is
> every angel.
> Ashes are in this generation's mouth, and in its spit is pus.

A wolf-bitch in a wasteland howling for the moon's
        listless whorishness;
The barbarians' halls are full to the brim, and
        church and altar abandoned,
Our vessel is drifting in the fog, and drunk are the
        crew and the captain.

In the heart of heaven's darkness, O Mary, set your Star,
And help us find the course back to His will by
        showing us your chart,
And descend among the tangled ropes, and put your
        hand to the tiller,
And pilot our rebellious craft into a heavenly harbour.[1]

The poem is one which belongs very much to its own decade. It
mirrors the hopelessness of the industrial south in the years of the
economic recession, and the first period of massive unem-
ployment. It reminds us that the twentieth-century Wales, which
we are seeing through the eyes of its poets, is a country which has
known terrible periods of economic failure, as well as times of
comparative affluence. No less from the literary and theological
point of view it is a poem characteristic of the moment when it was
written. Its opening echoes a line of T. S. Eliot from *The Rock*, and
the first stanza with its contrast between the hymn of Christ's
intercession, on the one hand, and the ideology of the Absolute on
the other tells us much about the way in which Gwenallt found it
possible to reaffirm his faith in Christ. Like many others of that
time he was in full reaction against the liberal protestantism of the
early twentieth century, which had been too ready to adopt the
grand language of Hegelian philosophy and see the whole history
of man as an unbroken if dialectical progress towards the
realization of the Absolute.

Such language sounded particularly empty and unreal to
people who had been confronted with the horrors of the First
World War, and who knew the frustration of the years of the
depression. It was vital for them to stress again the givenness of the
Christian revelation; to insist that all hinges on God's initiative,
not ours. Man is fallen, he stands in need of salvation. There is a
drama of revelation and redemption, not the gradual and

inevitable progress of human history to the heights. So it was, at this same time, that perhaps the greatest Protestant theologian since the Reformation, Karl Barth, reasserted the absolute primacy of the action of God and reinstated at the heart of Christian faith the classical doctrines of the Incarnation and the Atonement. In England his teaching was welcomed and received by theologians of the stature of Edwyn Hoskyns and Michael Ramsey, the future Archbishop of Canterbury. They incorporated it into a Catholic vision of Christianity in which the different traditions of western Christendom came together in a striking and persuasive synthesis. Michael Ramsey's first book, *The Gospel and the Catholic Church*, published in 1936 reveals a remarkable fusion of Barthian and Catholic elements on the part of a writer who was already also deeply influenced by his contacts with Eastern Orthodoxy. All this is part of the background to Gwenallt's writing, and it is very evident, for instance, in his great elegy for the Bangor theologian, J. E. Daniel. It is clear that Gwenallt had read widely in the theology of his time. He himself made a creative contribution to its movement of Catholic and Evangelical reconciliation. At the end of the poem we have been considering there comes the sudden invocation of Mary. One of the many surprises that Welsh poetry has in store for the English or American reader, is the discovery that the sense of the communion of saints is so strong that the practice of calling upon the saints for their prayers and their help seems to come naturally to quite a number of the poets. There is the example for instance of the Congregationalist Cynan's poem of invocation addressed to the eighteenth-century hymn-writer Ann Griffiths, or the Quaker Waldo's prayer to the Celtic saint of Nevern in Pembrokeshire, Brynach the Irishman. As we shall see, in the course of this chapter this faith in the communion of saints has powerful implications for our attitude towards the inescapable fact of death.

I

After the outspoken anger of Gwenallt it is instructive to turn to the work of a writer of our own time, who speaks of the situation in Wales, and more generally, as it confronts us today and has

confronted us for the last two decades. If Gwenallt can speak for
the thirties and the forties, Gwyn Thomas can speak for the
seventies and eighties. The quiet restraint of his work only
heightens our awareness of the writer's horror at his vision of the
world in which we live. I shall quote two poems: the first is from a
collection published in 1976, though as topical today as it was
then; a poem written after hearing a news item from Belfast. It has
at its head a quotation from the gospel of Luke (23.29). 'But Jesus
turning unto them said, Daughters of Jerusalem, weep not for me,
but weep for yourselves, and for your children.'

> Children.
> Little children playing –
> John and Joanne;
> And Andrew the baby,
> The little baby, with them.
>
> Between them, between the three of them
> There was a length of life
> Of ten years and six weeks
> John and Joanne
> And Andrew, the baby.
>
> And men came by
> Inside the iron and glass and plastic of their car
> Carrying guns,
> Bullets, fuse-wire,
> Black powder,
> With their hands already red with death;
> And men came by to destroy children:
> John and Joanne
> And Andrew, the baby.
>
> And then they went away,
> Back into the concrete and glass,
> Into the wounded city
> To eat, to sleep, to live
>
> As if there were not in their hearts
> The death of John, the death of Joanne

The death of Andrew, the little baby:
Children.

And above the grief of the congregation,
Above those who were
Bending over the dead
They were there again
Unfurling the banners of their wrath,
Those who can eat,
Who can sleep, who can live
After killing children.[2]

The second poem comes from a collection published more
recently and reflects a common experience in many parts of the
island of Britain, particularly outside the south-east. Again in its
directness and reticence it says much.

The factory's shutting down, and he's now fifty;
A feeling of an ending comes, like soot falling,
Dark about his heart,
And the future slams in his face.

A future on the dole in a poor place:
The son decides to join the army;
The daughter's looking for something in Birmingham,
Where his sister lives.

Houses for sale, shops closing down
And going to rack and ruin with those young men
Who take no pleasure in anything
But lounging about in pubs and breaking and destroying.
Even the chapel windows are full of holes,
And someone's been there painting on the walls,
PUNKS RULE O.K. and profanities.

And on the telly every day –
Between chocolate dreams –
There are pictures of killing, hungry children dying,
Vicious people snarling.

And a nasty feeling grows on him,

Like a spider moving on his neck,
That, soon, the whole show will be smashed.[3]

These two poems speak to us powerfully of two of the most
characteristic experiences of death in our time, the sudden violent
death which comes through urban terrorism, the slow quiet death
which comes with changing patterns of industrial life and activity.
Both are clearly related to the structures of a society which places
a much higher value on money than on human life, and in which
human considerations are therefore often given little priority. The
apathy and the despair of those who feel excluded from any real
participation in the growth and development of society is always
liable to break out in the petty violence of vandalism and
hooliganism; given appropriate conditions it can show itself in the
massive organized violence of the IRA and UVF in Belfast. This is
a fact we must acknowledge. The Christian poet will perhaps
want to say more than this. He cannot well say less. It is perhaps
this steadfast, honest facing of the facts of violence and death,
experienced and confronted at so many different levels, personal,
social, natural and global which is one of the keys to the capacity
of the Welsh poets of our time to go on and say that 'more' with
integrity and honesty. In the Christian scheme of things it is in
dying that Christ overcomes death.

This paradoxical assertion is indeed at the very heart of the
most exuberant of all traditional Christian affirmations of the
victory of the resurrection. In the Easternight service of the
Orthodox Church, one short hymn is repeated time and time
again. 'Christ has risen from the dead. By death he has trampled
down death, and to those in the tombs given life.' This conquest of
death by death is not a solitary exploit on the part of the Lord.
Precisely because he is the Lord, in whom all things hold together,
his death alters the whole fabric of our existence. All things were
changed by Christ's passion. It is the constant affirmation of
Christian worship in east and west alike. In Christ all creation is
raised up into the possibility of new life. In the coming of the Holy
Spirit, a communion, a sharing of life comes into being which
crosses over the gulf of death and makes this world one with the
world to come. Time and space are no longer barriers to

communion, they become its channels. Death itself is no longer supreme in human affairs. When we pray through Christ and in the Spirit we are caught up into his victory over death and enter into a communion of love and knowledge which unites us with those who are farthest from us.

This faith in the communion of saints is a part of the universal Christian inheritance of faith and experience. But it would be impossible to deny that it has received a very special expression in Celtic Christianity, not least in the tradition of Wales in our own century.

To discover this we shall start with a poem by Waldo Williams 'After the Silent Centuries' is one of the great poems in Welsh of this period. It is the work of a man who from being a Baptist had become a Quaker, and it was written to celebrate the Roman Catholic martyrs of Wales from the sixteenth and seventeenth centuries. It is a poem which was written almost fifty years ago when such acts of Christian recognition across deeply entrenched ecclesiastical barriers were less easily made than they are today, written in honour of those who had undergone red martyrdom, martyrdom of blood, by one who in his own life knew much of white martyrdom, the martyrdom of suffering freely accepted for the sake of Christ.

I knot their praises, for long centuries mute.
The core of all faith is one, it is splendid to meet
With souls one with the quick at Being's root.

Over my head they are there, they are one with the light
Where through the expanse peace gathers. When night
Veils the sky, each is a shining gap to my sight.

John Roberts of Trawsfynydd, priest to the needy,
In the dread plague shared out the bread of the journey,
Knowing the powers of the dark had come, and would break
    his body.

John Owen, the joiner, that many a servant concealed.
For the old communion his hand an unwearying shield,
Lest the plait be unravelled, and the beams of the great
    house yield.

Richard Gwyn smiled in their face at what they were at:
'I have sixpence towards your fine' – for he'd not
In the cause of his Master, price his life more than that.

They that ran light, I cannot reckon them all,
A company gathered together beyond the pits of hell:
Surely nothing can scatter them who paid the selfsame toll.

The last, quiet payment. World for world giving them,
For the Spirit to guide them giving that ultimate pain,
Giving a flower for his root, for his cradle a grain.

Torture did rack them, disembowelling rend,
Ere the sight where a ladder was given their souls to ascend
To the broad next morning of Golgotha, their blest Lord's
          world without end.

Welshmen, were you a nation, great would be the glory
These would have in your story.[4]

We turn back now from the sixteenth century to the sixth, to the most famous of all of Wales's saints, St David, and look at two poems of the mid century devoted to him. They are both quite long discursive poems and, for this reason, translate well. They treat their subject in very different ways. Gwenallt, who we shall consider first, writes of St David as altogether our contemporary. Indeed it is interesting to notice the references to the house Mass and the celebration facing the people, both very new experiments in Anglican circles at the time when this poem was written in the late 1940s, the moment when the worker-priest movement in France was arousing passionate interest in Britain. The poem as a whole, as with much of Gwenallt's work, makes its statement very clearly and directly. But it is full of touches which could be the subject of further comment. For instance, at a personal level, the words about the Christian being purified in the furnace, refer to the death of Gwenallt's own father. More theologically, the reference to 'the gospel and the altar' which Dewi takes with him is a typical expression of the concern for an Evangelical-Catholic fullness which we find throughout the mature poetry of this writer. The opening lines of the poem affirm a faith which is perhaps most strongly of all expressed in Eastern Christianity though it is certainly known in Catholicism too. It is clear that though he did not have many contacts with Orthodoxy, Gwenallt was not unaware of this fact.

There is no barrier between two worlds in the Church.
The Church militant on earth
Is one with Church triumphant in heaven,
And the saints are in this Church which is two in one.
They come to worship with us, our small congregation,
The saints our oldest ancestors
Who built Wales on the foundation
Of the Crib, the Cross and the Empty tomb.
And they go out as before to travel their old ways
And to evangelize Wales.
I have seen Dewi going from shire to shire like the gipsy of God,
With the gospel and the altar in his caravan;
He came to us in the colleges and schools
To show us the purpose of learning.
He went down into the pit with the coal miners
And shone his lamp on the coal face.
He put on the goggles of the steel worker, and the short grey
    overall
And showed the Christian being purified like metal in the
    furnace.
He brought the factory people into his disreputable Church
He carried the Church everywhere
Like a body with life and mind and will,
And he did small things and great.
He brought the Church into our homes,
Put the holy vessels on the kitchen table
With bread from the pantry and wine from the cellar,
And he stood behind the table like a tramp
So as not to hide from us the wonder of the sacrifice.
And after the Communion we had a talk round the fire
And he spoke to us of God's natural order,
The person, the family, the nation and the society of nations
And the cross which prevents us from making any of them
    into a god.
He said that God had made our nation
For his own purposes

And that its death would be a breach of that order.
Anger darkened his forehead as he castigated us
For licking the arse of the Saxon Leviathan
And allowing ourselves in his own country to be turned into
    Pavlov's dogs.
We besought his pardon, his grace and his keenness, asking him
To give the Lord Jesus Christ our poor congratulations
And to ask that we might come to be with him forever
When comes that longed for moment to bid the world Good
    Night.[5]

The poem gives an impressive account of Gwenallt's faith that the Gospel of Christ touches and renews the whole of human life, personal and social, intellectual and industrial. It clearly reflects his own boyhood in south Wales and the political and national concerns which were with him throughout his career. But none of those concerns, however important in themselves, can be taken to be an ultimate end. All can become idols unless seen under the judgement of the cross of Christ, in the light of his death and resurrection. Human life constantly needs to look beyond itself to something greater than we can know or formulate here. It only finds its ultimate fulfilment in the life of God. But all this is earthed, made close to us, seen and expressed in terms of this world. The sacramental presence of Christ is made known in ordinary kitchen bread, not in some paper-thin ecclesiastical wafer. God enters into the substance of our daily living, and this enables us to find him in all things, and finding him to make our way through all things into the mystery of the kingdom which is in the end beyond all our imagining or desiring. The presence of the saints with us, around us, is an embodied testimony to the reality of this transformation.

If Gwenallt's poem about 'St David' speaks of him as our contemporary, Saunders Lewis's poem on 'The Last Sermon of St David' takes us back into the period of the saint himself and into the time of his medieval biographers. The poet meditates on the fact that the saint's death-bed injunction to his disciples to do 'the little things' they had heard and seen in him is given us in the Welsh life written in the fourteenth century by the Anchorite of Llanddewibrefi, the place connected with one of the most famous episodes in St David's life, where he is said to have dominated the synod by the quality of his eloquence. It is not however found in this form in the life written in Latin two centuries earlier, towards the end of the eleventh century by Rhygyfarch, on which the Welsh version is in general based. Rhygyfarch had written in the period immediately after the Norman Conquest of England, when the Normans were penetrating deep into south Wales, and when two powerful Norman archbishops, Lanfranc and Anselm, were asserting the rights of Canterbury over the church in Wales in a way which their Anglo-Saxon predecessors had never done. It was a time of anxiety in the old Celtic centre of Llanbadarn Fawr where Rhygyfarch wrote, one of those moments which seemed to indicate the end of a whole age of church life and worship. The development of the cult of St David was one way in which people sought to strengthen their sense of national identity and tradition, at that moment.

But more than this, the poem centres on the extreme simplicity and sobriety of the message conveyed in the saint's last sermon, as contrasted with the combination of earthly and heavenly splendours which the medieval hagiographers ascribe to the moment of his death. As David dies the saints of Ireland and Wales gather to his death-bed. The angels come to receive the soul into heaven. The great monastic founder, renowned for the austerity of his way of life, an austerity to equal that of the monks of the Egyptian desert, the abbot who is descended from the royal line of Cunedda gives, in his last words, a message as simple and as gentle as that of St Thérèse of Lisieux or St Bernadette. Is this message with its exhortation to do the 'little things', a message which has lingered on through the centuries in oral tradition, handed on by word of mouth by the little people, the unimportant, despised people who have in fact lived by this word, kept the faith, done the little things, and in and through darkness found the light which has enabled them to be joyful? Saunders Lewis is writing a poem here, not an academic exercise in literary history. But only those who have no knowledge of the tenacity of oral tradition in Celtic-speaking communities both in Wales and Ireland will be altogether scornful of the suggestion. St David had rooted himself in the hearts and minds of his people.

It was a strange sermon that David preached
After the Sunday mass before the first of March
To the crowd that had come to him to mourn his dying;
'Brothers and sisters, be joyful
Keep the faith and do the little things
That you saw and heard from me.
And I shall walk the way our fathers went,
Fare thee well,' said David
'And never more shall we meet again.'
That is how the anchorite of Llanddewibrefi records the
          sermon.
A fuller version than the Latin of Rhygyfarch,
And it may be that it was from the recollections in the
memories of rustic believers
Who had wandered the banks of the Teifi like prayers
Slipping one by one through the fingers of the centuries,
That the version the anchorite put in his parchment was
          found.
No sunset was ever more imperial
Than the journeying of David from the senate of Brefi
To his death in the church and the vale of roses.
A week before this day, in the morning service,
The proclamations of his release were announced to him
By a choir of angels; and by an angel
Was the news spread through the churches of Wales and the
          churches
Of gentle Ireland. There was an assembly at Saint David's,
The saints of two isles came to bury their saint;
The city was filled with tears and weeping
And wailing, woe that the earth does not swallow us,
     Woe that the sea does not cover the land, woe that the
          mighty mountains
Do not fall upon us.
And the first of March
To the weeping church came the victorious church,
And the sun, and the nine orders of heaven, and songs and
          perfumes:
David went from wonder to wonder to his God.

That is how Rhygyfarch records the story
In the hour of his heaviness in Llanbadarn Fawr,

In the hour of the trouble of the canons and the anguish of a
    country,
With the old writings of David in his chest
And the old chronicles and relics of the clerks,
The remnant of the greatness that had been and that had
    been dear,
In the sorrowful cloister, in the reminiscent cell.
And likewise, two centuries later, is the story
According to the anchorite who copied it by the hill
Where Brefi's senate was, and the feet of the saint and the
    miracle.
But neither miracle nor angel was found in David's sermon
After the Sunday mass before the first of March
To the crowd that had come there to mourn his dying,
Nor the summoning of the cloister as witness to the glories;
But an exhortation to the humble ways, be joyful
And keep the faith and do the little things
That you saw and heard from me.
To historians the rule of David has been awesome
And the Egyptian whip of his abstinence and the heavy yoke,
The lord of saints, great-grandson of Cunedda and the
    purple.
But his last words, the sermon that nestled in the memories
Of those who prayed on the banks of the Teifi through
    centuries,
Of terror, through war, under the scowl of the vulture
    castles,
Through the ages when the grasshopper was a burden,
They are the words of a maid, the gentleness of a nun,
The 'little way' of Teresa towards the purification and the
    union,
And the way of the poor maid who saw Mary at Lourdes.[6]

In these last lines there is a remarkable insight into one of the
paradoxical characteristics of Christian sanctity. When a man or
woman begins to grow into some measure of human and spiritual
wholeness, it can sometimes happen that they seem to acquire
some of the characteristics which appear to be opposite to their
natural temperament, or which belong to the opposite sex. The
woman acquires the firmness, the resolution, the discernment of
the man. The man acquires the gentleness, the tenderness, the

insight of the woman. Humankind as a whole, male and female, is created in the image of God. In each one of us something of the opposite sex is latent. The one who follows the monastic way, a way which renounces the fullness of marriage, is sometimes enabled to find within himself the complementarity and fullness of male and female, which is given in another form in the union of husband and wife. Saunders Lewis's juxtaposition of David and Thérèse, meant, in a way which is altogether typical of him, to surprise and disconcert us, reveals a depth of intuition into the ways of holiness which is also characteristic of this amazingly perceptive poet.

The theme of the communion of saints is one which meets us in many places in modern Welsh poetry. It links with the sense of the unity of tradition, of the presence of the past, which runs through the whole. It is an essential part of that severely threatened thing, the sense of national identity. 'What is love of country?' Waldo asks in his poem 'What is man?' and he replies 'Keeping house, amidst a cloud of witnesses'. It can also take a more personal turn in the form of a poem written in praise of some known and loved person who has recently died. These poems, as we shall suggest in the second half of this book, have a function unexpectedly similar to the icons of the saints in Eastern Orthodoxy. They celebrate and proclaim the light of God shining out in the face of a particular man or woman, and allow us to enter into communion with that light. But perhaps the poem which most of all sums up this feeling about the communion of saints as a whole, is another work of Gwenallt's which is called simply 'Wales'. Here the theme of the interpenetration of grace and nature, which we considered in the previous chapter, finds classical and luminous expression.

> Martyrs' dust through countless ages
> And the saints lie in thy breast,
> Thou didst give them breath and being,
> Thou didst call them to thy rest.
>
> On thy roads are seen the footprints
> Made by angels from above,
> And the Holy Ghost has settled
> In thy branches like a dove.

Bards have heard in winds and breezes
Sighs of sacrificial pain,
Deep within thy darkest forests
The Rood Tree doth still remain.

His resurrection was thy springtime,
Thy summer was His triumph green,
And in the winter of thy mountains
Tabernacles have been seen.

Providential dews and raindrops
On thy fields of oat and corn,
And His glory on the harness
Of thy horses in the morn.

Thy ships have sped o'er many waters,
Laden with a precious prize,
Their sails have borne across the ocean
Calvary's richest merchandise.

For himself thy God has chosen
Thee to love Him evermore,
And his covenant is written
On the lintel of thy door.

Thy saints are clothed in morning radiance
They love thee, thy joy and pride,
Like a mother-bird thou callest
Warm beneath thy wing they hide.[7]

This is a poem which presupposes a deep confidence in the holiness of the earth. The saints of this land are the sons and daughters of this land. They are also the sons and daughters of God; rooted in the earth they have risen up into an eternal inheritance. Yet the life which they have received from God, the eternal life in which they now rejoice, is not something apart from, unrelated to the life which they have lived and shared here on earth. That life in all its human fullness and fragility has been nurtured and sustained by this particular corner of the earth's surface. It has been shaped by these particular places which have

themselves become holy in a special way because they have been
known and loved by these particular people. It has been sustained
by this particular language, and by the wealth of experience and
understanding which that language has conveyed.

All human life is holy since it is a gift from God, and when it is
lived in conscious communion with him then that holiness
becomes manifest. All this earth is holy since it is God's gift to us, a
gift to be received and offered back to him in praise and
thanksgiving. When we do this then its holiness becomes manifest.
It is ours to cherish or destroy, to disfigure or transfigure. The face
of the earth has been terribly disfigured by the sin of man.
Humanity shares in that disfigurement. It has brought us down to
death and, at this very moment, this earth is threatened with the
sudden death of a nuclear holocaust or the slow death caused by
pollution and abuse. But it is this death which Christ has
destroyed by accepting it into himself; it is this sin which Christ
has taken away, by accepting it into his own body and taking it to
the cross. So when we confess our faith in the communion of saints,
we go on at once to confess our faith in the forgiveness of sins and
the life everlasting. These things go together.

The vision of a transfigured universe, a world alive with the
energies and glory of God, of which the Welsh tradition is so full, is
not to be separated from a belief in the forgiveness of sins, that
creative gift of God which through the cross can bring light out of
darkness. This communion is a sharing of holy people and of holy
things. 'The things of God for the people of God', as we declare at
the moment of communion in the Eucharistic celebration. This is
what Gwenallt is speaking about here. This is what lies at the
heart of that offering of praise and thanksgiving which recreates
an unblemished world.

II

The Tradition Considered

The Place of Ann Griffiths

At the end of the lecture on Ann Griffiths which he gave at Newtown during the National Eisteddfod in 1965, a lecture which evidently made an indelible impression on many of those who heard it, Saunders Lewis said,

> In the religious debate which has been going on in the press and through the medium of the radio in Wales for the last year or more, I am in complete sympathy with the starting point of Professor J. R. Jones, viz. that the crisis which is weighing upon Christians and ex-Christians today is not a crisis of guilt, but of doubt as to whether life has any meaning at all.

For Ann Griffiths, as he had argued throughout the lecture, the question of forgiveness, of reconciliation, of the wiping out of guilt, however important it may be, is not the first thing.

As to what comes first she has not the slightest doubt,

> .   Diolch byth, a chanmil diolch
>   Diolch tra bo yno'i chwyth
>   Am fod gwrthrych i'w addoli . . .

(Thanks for ever, and a hundred thousand thanks, thanks while there is breath in me, that there is an object of worship . . .)

Ann is a poet putting off her shoes from her feet, because the ground on which she stands at Llanfihangel-yng-Ngwynfa is holy ground. Where there is an object of worship, there cannot be a moment's doubt that life has an eternal meaning, that meaning is everywhere in the universe.[1]

It is only when it is clear that the eternal, the absolute, the infinite exist and can be known and loved in this world that the incessant flux of happenings in space and time can have meaning and direction, can become *history*; and we remember that behind the Welsh word for *meaning*, *ystyr* there stands *historia*, a story which has a beginning and an end.

In the quarter of a century which has passed since that lecture was given, the threat of meaninglessness has not diminished in our civilization. The feeling that human life, whether we think of the individual or of a whole society, does not make a coherent story has become stronger and more pervasive; it can be seen in the very forms which our literature is taking. In his book on the life and message of Carl Gustav Jung, Laurens van der Post discusses this phenomenon at some length. He comments on our situation, in which too often

> there is no discernible meaning for man in what he is asked to do, and no overall and honourable value in the evolution of the society or culture to which he belongs to compensate him for the meaninglessness which affects him in his personal work and condition of being ... The human heart, as history proves, I believe, can endure anything except a state of meaninglessness. Without meaning it dies like a fish without water on the sands of a wasteland beach.[2]

And in the same book van der Post gives a vivid illustration of the truth of this remark, speaking of the bushmen people of Southern Africa and their reluctance to disclose their traditional stories to outsiders.

> I realised that the story was their most precious possession and that they were protecting it as best they could. They knew how dangerous it was to let a foreigner, above all a white foreigner, in on the secret of their stories. He might destroy them, either by making fun of them, or using them against them ... Without a story of its own, no culture, society or personality could survive.[3]

What is true in Africa is true also in other continents, not least here in Europe. What is the story which we have lost, and what part in it has Ann Griffiths? What is her place within the story of Wales, of Britain, of Christendom and humankind?

In one sense it is easy to answer the question in regard to Ann; what was her place? Saunders Lewis has already answered it for us; Llanfihangel-yng-Ngwynfa, the parish in which she spent much the greater part of her life; or still more precisely, Dolwar Fach, the farmhouse in which she was born, from which she was married, in which she died. Her story is a notable part of the larger story of the Methodist revival in eighteenth-century Wales. Ann Griffiths's place on the surface of the globe is as clearly delimited as is the brief space which she occupies in time, 1776 to 1805, from the Declaration of American Independence to the Battle of Trafalgar. And to that narrow space and time there corresponds the very slender character of what remains of her for us, a handful of letters existing in copies made by a friend and about thirty hymns handed down by oral tradition.

And if we ask what kind of a place it was in which she lived, we should have to reply that by any ordinary reckoning it was a small and marginal one. In terms of the social conventions of her times and within the confines of her own neighbourhood Ann could have been considered, as Saunders Lewis calls her, 'yn gryn dywysoges, very much a lady'.[4] But in the Britain of Jane Austen, a Welsh tenant-farmer's daughter would have had little recognition. And beyond such considerations there is of course the further aspect of the matter which we have not yet directly confronted. Ann lived and spoke and sang and wrote in Welsh. And as we know, from a passage in the mid-nineteenth-century government report on education, known as the Blue Books, which Saunders Lewis made famous by his use of it in his lecture on 'The Fate of the Language',

> Whether in the country or among the furnaces, the Welsh el-
> ement is never found at the top of the social scale . . . Equally
> in his new as in his old home, his language keeps him under
> the hatches, being one in which he can neither acquire nor
> communicate the necessary information. It is a language of

old-fashioned agriculture, of theology, and of simple rustic
life, while all the world about him is English . . . His superiors
are content simply to ignore his existence . . . He is left to live
in an under-world of his own, and the march of society goes
completely over his head.[5]

These words come from a document written in the 1840s only a
generation after Ann's death. In them we feel the full force of
nineteenth-century utilitarianism in relation to education, as well
as of the feelings of the English about the value of the Welsh
language. We notice the contrast between the value put on
'information' as opposed to the value put on 'theology'. As Dr
Tudur Jones perceptively remarks of the attitudes revealed here,

> Answers to the question Why are superseded by technology.
> People should be taught in secular matters. Practical,
> scientific and technological knowledge is the key to mastering
> the world, and therefore the key to moulding the future.[6]

No one could pretend that the growth of such knowledge has
been or is unimportant in the last two centuries. But it is the one-
sided development of such knowledge at the expense of all other
forms of knowing which is one of the principal factors in the crisis
of meaning and meaninglessness which besets us today. No society
can devote its energy and attention exclusively to the question
'how', to the almost total neglect of the question 'why', without
suffering mortal consequences. The key to the future now lies in a
recovery of a sense of direction, not in the amassing of more and
more information. While it is evident that the Welsh language has
suffered from the restrictions placed on its use, the fact that it has
been comparatively little used for technological and scientific
purposes may have something to do with its evocative power and
with the remarkable flowering of Christian and theological poetry
which we have seen in Wales during the last fifty years.

Meanwhile the English-speaking world remains 'content
simply to ignore' the very existence of this Welsh tradition. As I
have repeatedly made the pilgrimage to Dolwar Fach I have
more than once reflected on how surprised my predecessors in
Oxford or Canterbury would have been to know that I was going

to pay homage at the house of a farmer's daughter in a remote corner of Welsh-speaking Wales. But it is not only your unheeding Englishman who is likely to ask, 'Can any good come out of Dolwar Fach?' I remember a Welsh-speaking Welshman, a graduate of the University of Oxford, who was frankly in-credulous when shown the theological quality of Ann's writing. 'How could it be, how can she have known such things?' To allow that, in any sense, Ann's position can be central in the history of Christian faith and devotion, and in the religious story of this island, Prydain Fawr, demands considerable alterations in our usual way of seeing things.

The clue as to the nature of those alterations can again be found in the words of Saunders Lewis which we quoted at the beginning, 'the ground on which she stands at Llanfihangel-yng-Ngwynfa is holy ground.' What does this mean? It is important to say in the first place, that it does not imply a claim for ethical perfection on behalf of Ann. That she struggled to live a life according to her faith and vision is abundantly clear from her letters; that it was a real struggle is also evident. What the outcome of that struggle was day by day, we cannot know in detail, though the tone and quality of both her prose and her verse suggest that she knew much indeed of that purity of heart, which as Kierkegaard tells us, is to will one thing. But the first point about holiness is that it is what belongs to God; it is a word which we use to speak about the transcendence of God, and yet of that transcendence com-municating itself, making itself known amongst men. One of the rare acknowledged saints of modern Anglicanism, Edward King, Bishop of Lincoln (1885–1910) says 'surprise is the motto of the saints', the surprise, the unexpectedness of this unforeseen encounter of man with God.[7] This is a word which we may well apply to Ann; surprise, amazement, *rhyfedd*. How surprised we are at the heights and depths of her vision; and how surprised she would have been at the thought of professors in the university and ministers of the Established Church solemnly pondering over the text of her hymns.

To speak of holiness in the Christian tradition is therefore to speak of what belongs to God in immediate reference to what belongs to humankind. It is to hint at unexpected capacities in human life, capacities which too often seem to be almost wholly unrealized, but which spring to life once the Spirit of God touches the human spirit and sets it on fire with a divine longing. It was this which people saw in Nansi Thomas. Or as Morris Davies puts it in his *Cofiant* of 1856, in words which surely reflect the memories of her contemporaries, no less than the evidence of her hymns, 'Her longing was ardent, passionate, heavenly; her rejoicing and delight [in the things of God] sometimes almost unbelievable.'[8]

As she sang

> O am dreiddio i'r adnabyddiaeth
>   O'r unig wir a'r bywiol Dduw
> I'r fath raddau a fo'n lladdfa
>   I ddychmygion o bob rhyw;. . .

(O to penetrate into the knowledge of the one true and living God, to such a degree as might be death to imaginings of every kind . . .)

or again

> O am gael ffydd i edrych
>   Gyda'r angylion fry
> I drefn yr iechydwriaeth
>   Dirgelwch ynddi sy;
> Dwy natur mewn un person
>   Yn anwahanol mwy
> Mewn purdeb heb gymysgu
>   Yn berffaith hollol trwy.

(O to have faith to look with the angels above into the plan of salvation, the mystery that is in it, two natures in one person, inseparable henceforth, in purity without confusion, perfect through and through.)

Yet as we see in these lines the expression of that longing is at the same time intensely intellectual. As Morris Davies remarks, 'Not heat without light, nor light without heat, but the two together.'[9] There is in her a combination of clarity of vision with depth of feeling which brings together the two sides of human nature in a remarkable unity. And that unity itself springs out of an even higher and more mysterious union of two in one. For the object of her desire is that one in whom man and God are inseparably brought together, for all eternity. She herself aspires to a similar union and communion as she is drawn into fellowship with her Lord and Saviour.

> Tragwyddol anwahanol undeb
> A chymundeb â fy Nuw.

(Eternal, inseparable union and communion with my God.)

As Pantycelyn exclaims also,

> Pa feddyliau uwch eu deall
> A gaf ynof fi fy hun,
> Wrth ystyried bod y Duwdod
> Perffaith pur a minnau'n un?
> Dyma gwlwm
> Nad oes iaith a'i dyd i maes.

(What thoughts above understanding shall I have within me when I consider that the perfect pure Godhead and I are made one? There is a knot which there is no language to express.)

The life and vision of such a person binds heaven and earth together into one, as Cynan declares in his poem addressed to Santes Ann, speaking of 'the inseparable union which now exists between Dolwar Fach and the great Resurrection'.

> Trwy'r anwahanol undeb sydd yn awr
> Rhwng Dolwar Fach a'r Atgyfodiad Mawr.[10]

Or as T. S. Eliot puts it in *Murder in the Cathedral*,

> Wherever a saint has dwelt . . .
>   There is holy ground and the sanctity
> shall not depart from it

> Though armies trample over it, though
> sightseers come with guidebooks looking
> over it. . . .
> From such ground springs that which
> forever renews the earth
> Though it is for ever denied.[11]

Here is the intersection of the timeless with time, the point at
which heaven and earth are reconciled, and unity brought in
between the littleness of man and the infinity and eternity of God.

It is this meeting of our universe of space and time with
something greater than space and time which gives to our world a
direction and a meaning, a sense of an ending. 'From such a
ground springs that which forever renews the earth, / Though it is
forever denied.' Where there is an object of worship, an object
who himself unites the ultimate with the conditional, God with
man, there it is clear 'that life has an eternal meaning, and that
meaning is everywhere in the universe'. Heaven and earth are full
of God's glory, shot through with the energies of his creative love.

I

We have made our affirmation, such as it is, of the centrality of
Ann Griffiths. It is a centrality which depends upon the fact that in
H. A. Hodges's words 'her whole vision of life and being is less
man-centred and more God-centred than most people's', and so it
is a centrality which will primarily seem plausible to those who are
themselves seeking to find their way towards a God-centred vision
of the universe. And we have seen that this God-centred vision is
of a peculiar nature, for it is not a vision which degrades or
belittles what is human. Quite the reverse. It is a vision of the
human as created for union with God, and entering into that
union through Christ and in the Holy Spirit; a vision which
literally rescues humanity from the threat of meaninglessness and
absurdity which seems to engulf us whenever we seek to assert our
own centrality apart from God.

But having made such a claim, we may still be inclined to ask
whether there is not some element of exaggeration here; how in
reality can these things be? On the question of exaggeration I

should like to appeal explicitly to the judgement of H. A. Hodges. Herbert Hodges was a silent, retiring man, a philosopher by profession and a sceptic by natural temperament. It was not in his nature to go beyond the evidence. A man of very wide reading with a great delight in things beautiful, he had a mind which insisted on questioning everything. A friend of his once remarked that what the world needs nowadays are 'sceptical mystics'. It was a good description of him; his last book was provisionally entitled 'Thoughts of a Sceptical Believer', his Gifford Lectures are called 'God beyond Knowledge'. Here undoubtedly was one of the things which attracted him to Ann; not that she can be called a sceptic but, without question, she was a thinker. She longed to penetrate into the mysteries of faith and she used her powers of reflection constantly to go further, to go beyond the formulations and the words she employed to the reality which lies beyond them.

This movement of thought, for Ann as a believer, for Hodges as a philosophical theologian, did not involve any loss of intellectual accuracy or precision, 'mysticism' in the pejorative sense of that word, in which the 'i' and the 'y' have changed places. Quite the reverse; let anyone who is in doubt read the lucid, sensitive pages of Hodges's introduction to the little book *Homage to Ann Griffiths*, which must be almost the last thing that he wrote, and weigh the thought and love which lies behind them. See for instance how he speaks of her use of paradoxes.

Her frequent emphasis on the paradoxes of the Christian story has often been remarked on as a feature of her literary style. It is so, but it is also more. Ann is a good hand at an epigram, and we can hardly doubt that she enjoys surprising us sometimes, but it is not done as a display of skill. It is her way of bringing us into her own state of astonishment at the inherent wonders of the Faith. These wonders can be seen and Ann sees them, on three distinct levels. First comes wonder in the sense of sheer surprise, and the Christian story is full of surprises which Ann delights to savour and exhibit to us. But second, wonder may mean a mingling of awe and admiration, such as we feel on contemplating the divine wisdom, love and power. In Addison's phrase which Wesley borrowed we are

'lost in wonder, love and praise'. And third, wonder may
mean the recognition of a mystery, an incomprehensibility,
such as we always find in the long run when we look into the
being of God and his actions towards us. Ann is filled with
wonder in all these three senses even in this life; and heaven to
her means living in the midst of a sea of wonders.[12]

There already his assessment of her is implicit; his sense of the
depth to be found in these apparently unstudied hymns, of the
insight which she has not only into the images and doctrines of
Scripture but into the rationale lying behind them, her constant
sense of delight and wonder before the inexhaustible being of
God, and the interplay of love and knowledge which constantly
leads her further on. And Hodges goes on to discuss her way of
speaking about heaven, comparing her with Gregory of Nyssa,
and his belief 'that the life even of the glorified is not a static
condition of finished achievement but a perpetual reaching
forward (*epektasis*) to explore the Inexhaustible. We may take it',
he adds, 'that Ann knew nothing of St Gregory of Nyssa, but she
shares his insight . . .'[13] It did not seem inappropriate to compare
the farmer's daughter with one of the greatest of the eastern
Fathers.

And here we have sharply placed before us the question of
Ann's sources, in some ways the most puzzling of the questions as
to the 'how' of her achievement. Where could she have got her
grasp of theology, the confidence with which she handles the
terms of classical Christology, for instance, 'two natures in one
person, inseparable henceforth, in purity without confusion,
perfect through and through'? Interesting light is thrown on the
social and intellectual background of Ann in some of the papers
published in the volume edited by Dyfnallt Morgan, not least in
that of Professor Geraint Gruffydd which points to the importance
of the Puritan influences in her work.[14] Professor Bobi Jones has
argued that she almost certainly knew the Welsh translation of
Richard Baxter's book *The Saint's Everlasting Rest*. I find his
argument on this point most persuasive. In such a book she would
have been in touch with one of the greatest and most wide-
reaching of seventeenth-century Puritan writers. Nor should we

underestimate the theological and spiritual quality of the teaching given by the two leading figures in the Calvinistic Methodism of north Wales in her time, Thomas Charles of Bala and Thomas Jones of Denbigh. In the writing of the latter, we have a combination of scholarship with devotion which in its own way is as remarkable as Ann's. Neither should we forget the importance of the Book of Common Prayer, not only for Ann Griffiths but for the formation of the whole of the first two generations of the Methodist movement in Wales. There she would have met texts from the classical period of Christian thinking, the Te Deum, or the Athanasian Creed. There she would have become accustomed to the use of the Scriptures in the context of prayer, and to the constant recitation of the Psalms. It is recorded that her own extemporary prayers were often brief. Is this perhaps a sign of the influence of the Prayer Book collects? To someone with her ear for rhythm, their noble brevity could have been strongly attractive.

But when all is said, none of these things will altogether account for Ann's greatness. As Gordon Rupp remarks in an essay on the study of Luther,

> The exciting thing about human beings, and a reason for the historical study of great men (and women), is to seek the 'X' in their equation, the point at which they cease to be explained by heredity and environment and the thought world of their contemporaries.[15]

And certainly this is the case with Ann Griffiths. While it is true that she cannot be understood apart from Welsh Methodism, a phenomenon in itself not easily explicable in terms of early eighteenth-century Wales, there is a quality in her which lifts her above nearly all her contemporaries, a quality which in the attentive reader awakens echoes of other strands of Christian tradition than those with which she could have been familiar. I take one quotation from her letters.

> That word is on my mind tonight. 'Go forth, O ye daughters of Zion, and behold King Solomon with the crown wherewith his mother crowned him in the day of his espousals, and in the day of the gladness of his heart.' I think there is a high and

peculiar calling for all who have part in the covenant to leave
their own ceiled houses to see their King wearing the crown of
thorns and the purple robe. It is a marvel to me to think who it
is that was on the cross – he whose eyes are as a flame of fire
piercing through heaven and earth in a single glance, unable
to see his creatures, the work of his hands. My mind is too
overwhelmed to say anything more on the matter.

Who is this who writes with such authority? Where does she get
such authority from?

II

I have said earlier that I believe Ann's greatness is only to be truly
appreciated if we think of her in terms of holiness, of some decisive
intersection of the timeless with time which takes place in and
around her years at Dolwar. She herself became convinced that
her insight into the faith came from God, and the believing reader
may come to the same conclusion. But to say this does not in itself
dispense us from trying to understand a little more of how it
happens. How is it that such a figure is at once a part of a
tradition, is indebted to predecessors in a regular historical
sequence and yet somehow transcends the tradition, is rooted in a
particular environment and yet grows beyond it? Here there are
interesting analogies between a literary and a religious tradition
which may help to illuminate both. Some of our difficulties in
understanding may be caused by a too uncritical view of the
linear nature of time, and the linear development of a tradition or
of a single life in time. If there are in fact moments of intersection
in which time is open on to something greater than itself, then
such moments may perhaps embody a fullness in which many
things from past and future are gathered together and made
accessible to one another. We may think of moments in the life of
an individual in which the whole future course of events seems
given and decided in an instant of vision.

> I made no vows, but vows
> Were then made for me; bond unknown to me

Was given, that I should be, else sinning greatly,
A dedicated spirit.[16]

We may think of moments in the life of a people or a civilization in which great issues are worked out in a brief spell of years. In the English literary tradition, how much of what is to follow is already given in principle in those astonishing fifty years between 1350 and 1400 which mark the first emergence of the modern language. In his monumental study of the thought of S. T. Coleridge, Thomas McFarland writes,

> We too often think of development as a kind of progress up a series of steps, the improvement of one's position by the abandonment of a previous position. Actually the word implies an unwrapping of something already there. Its sister words in German and French suggest the same psychological truth: *Entwicklung* implies an unwrapping, *épanouissement* a flowering from a bud.[17]

We might add that the same is true of the Welsh word *datblygu*.

If this is true in a general way, it is certainly true of a religious tradition, and we are thinking in this case specifically of the Christian one. All is given in principle at the very beginning, whether we take the thirty years of Nazareth and Galilee or the ninety years of the Apostolic Age. Indeed we may say with Pantycelyn and a host of other Welsh hymn-writers that all is given in 'one afternoon'. And as such a tradition passes through the centuries it can show powers of recovery which startle and bewilder us. Its powers can lie dormant for many centuries before suddenly bursting into new flame. From the age of the saints to the eighteenth century in Wales is a long way in terms of ordinary chronology. Perhaps on another scale there is an unexpected closeness.

Furthermore it is clear that a spiritual tradition can flourish in outwardly unpromising circumstances and with little of the means of support which we would normally think necessary. I take an example from another part of the Christian world, the sudden outburst of fresco-painting in the sixteenth century in Moldavia, which produced painted churches of a quality not surpassed in all Christendom. Where did they come from? Why did they appear at that moment in an isolated province scarcely holding its own against the Turks? How did it happen that themes and images from Byzantine hymnography from texts written a thousand or so years earlier here find such eloquent visual expression? How did the painters succeed in synthesizing typically eastern and typically western elements of design in a single and harmonious unity?[18] The answers which we can give are again in the end unsatisfying. We can point to the continuity of the Orthodox Church, the strength of its liturgical life preserving the structures of the faith through the centuries, a function performed at least to some degree by the Prayer Book in post-Reformation Wales. We can point to other factors which are as important, though less easily discernible. Through the brilliance and transparency of the Moldavian frescoes we can see something of the depth of insight given in the prayer of the Romanian monastic communities, greatly influenced as they were by the hesychastic movement on Mount Athos. Speaking of Romania in this period Olivier Clement says 'one has the impression of a monastic civilisation; not a monasticism which constitutes itself into a kind of world of its own . . . but a monasticism which acts as a ferment, in a genuine osmosis with a whole people, which inspires a whole culture.'[19] In the burning images of Pantycelyn and Ann we may detect the force of prayer and faith which animated the early years of the Methodist revival in Wales, and which gave such power to the preaching and the singing which characterized that movement as a whole. In Wales too a whole people was touched, a new civilization formed by the power of this prayer. In Wales, as in Moldavia, in areas geographically remote from the main centres of the Christian world, in times apparently unpropitious, works of a classical significance were produced, works which from henceforth assume a central place in the growth of the tradition.

As we worked together on the study of Ann's writings, Hodges and I found ourselves saying from time to time; here are things which belong not only to Welsh-speaking Wales but to the whole world, things of a reconciling importance for Christians of many traditions, and indeed for men and women of other faiths as well.

This conviction has been greatly strengthened over the years as it has become clear that Ann's works arouse an equally enthusiastic response in Roman Catholics as in Evangelicals, in Orthodox as in members of the Church in Wales. I think of the response which they have evoked when presented in certain monasteries and convents in France. Such writings speak to the future as well as to the past, and they speak out of the heart of that common tradition of faith and experience which the divisions between Christians have too often masked from us. They speak of our human capacity for God, and of the way in which men and women may be visited by transcendent powers. They are formed within a certain doctrinal framework, but they are able to speak beyond it, to address all who seek to understand our journey of exploration into God, and the still more mysterious reality of God's search for humankind. And what is said here of Ann would surely be in a measure true of those who shared with her in that great stirring of life, spiritual and personal, intellectual and social, which we call the Methodist movement, whether in Wales or in England.

Let us turn for a moment to the greatest of all the singers of the movement in Wales, William Williams Pantycelyn (1717–91), to feel something of the force of the impact of the divine.

> Fflam o dân o ganol nefoedd
>   Yw, ddisgynnodd yma i'r byd
> Tân i losgi'm natur gyndyn
>   Tân a leinw f'eang fryd;
>   Hwn ni ddiffydd
> Tra parhao Duw mewn bod.

(It is a flame of fire from midmost heaven that came down hither into the world, fire that will burn up my stubborn nature, fire that will fill the breadth of my mind; it will not fail while God remains in being.)

'Infinite beauty and unquenchable love; that is Pantycelyn's joy, that is what is meant by "enjoyment" of God,' wrote Hodges commenting on that verse. In another place he speaks of Pantycelyn's 'overwhelming sense of God as infinite being and

infinite beauty'. It is the same with Ann; take the verse which is
said to have come to her as she rode back over the hills after
communion at Bala, and which speaks of repose more than of
movement, or rather embodies the reconciliation of the two.

> O ddedwydd awr tragwyddol orffwys
>   Oddiwrth fy llafur yn fy rhan
> Yng nghanol môr o ryfeddodau
>   Heb weled terfyn byth na glan;
> Mynediad helaeth byth i bara
>   O fewn trigfannau Tri yn Un;
> Dŵr i nofio heb fynd trwyddo
>   Dyn yn Dduw a Duw yn ddyn.

(O blessed hour of eternal rest from my labour in my lot, in
the midst of a sea of wonders with never a sight of an end or a
shore; abundant freedom of entrance ever to continue into the
dwelling places of the Three in One, water to swim in, not to
be passed through, man as God, and God as man.)

Here are affirmations based on knowledge, which respond in an
overwhelming way to that human situation of near despair which
we considered at the beginning of this chapter. They are
affirmations of the possibility of our humanity, of our capacity to
know some ultimate joy, some final fulfilment, which must stir us
by their depth and certainty. They are statements which were
made not so far away and not so long ago by a man living in a farm
house near Llanymddyfri, by a woman in a little house in a fold in
the Berwyns.

If these statements are of a universal significance and belong of
right to the whole world, none the less their home, the place of
their origin is in Wales, and it is in Wales that they are still most
immediately apprehended and lived. Certainly the practice of
hymn-singing has diminished, the number of those in church and
chapel has greatly decreased; in some ways we find that the
language and images of the eighteenth century have become
opaque to us; all that is true. But still the hymns can sound out
with fervour; they can still embody the faith and vision of a
people. In out-of-the-way places the experience lives on and

shows unexpected powers of recovery. Those who come from outside Wales should note these things with attention, should recognize the immense value of what has hitherto been hidden from us, must acknowledge that in the 'underworld' of which the Blue Books spoke so scornfully ('his superiors are content simply to ignore his existence') there existed and exist resources spiritual, intellectual, human and social of urgent value to us all in the late twentieth century. What that recognition would involve for the radical readjustment of the relations between England and Wales, and for a wholly new understanding of the importance of the Welsh language and the Welsh tradition, is not the subject of this chapter. But that there should be some far-reaching consequences should be plain for all to see.

Note

In 1967, when the English translation of Saunders Lewis's lecture on Ann was first published in *Sobornost*, I sent a copy to David Jones, at that time living in Harrow. In a letter dated 3 September of that year he wrote.

I have, of course, heard about Ann Griffiths from various Welsh friends but it takes a person such as Saunders to really make plain, in his inimitable way, her real significance – the extraordinary phenomenon she presents suddenly appearing within that most unlikely religious milieu of late 18th Cent. Calvinistic Wales. Not that I know much of the actualities of that period of Welsh history, nor for *that* matter, much about 'mystics' – in fact very little. But from what I've been told by Welshmen of Ann G. I've not been able to get more than the vaguest idea. But Saunders certainly seems to put his finger on the essentials of her insights, her particular approach, her haecceity, or however one says it – for, as I note Professor Hodges says in his article, the characteristic attitude or preoccupation of mystics varies – in some it is the contemplation of the Passion for example.

Then in a note in the margin he adds,

I should rather *expected* [sic] there to have been more than one Welsh Catherine Emmerich. But apparently not. But I myself have heard in my childhood, a clergyman, a Welsh-speaking friend of my father's preach a sermon in English on a Good Friday that had very considerable evocative concentration on the Instruments of the Passion, and moreover he did not fail to connect the immolation on the Tree with the oblation at the Supper, though he was *decidedly* protestant theologically. But though this was over sixty years ago I can still hear him say with a *very* Welsh inflection: 'He *drank* the Cup'.

A week later on 11 September he wrote again, and again referred to the lecture of Saunders.

I suppose had Ann Griffiths' brief life been lived not in the uplands of Powys but in some land such as that of Sister Elizabeth of the Trinity of the Dijon Carmel whom you mention in your letter as being near Ann in thought, she might by now be known as Beata Anna de Dolwar – or however they'd say 'of Dolwar' in liturgical Latin! anyway Anna Wenfydedig o Ddolwar or something of that sort in the tongue of the land – don't know.

It has occurred to me while reading Saunders' thing that if Dolwar means what, in my amateur and guess work fashion I take it might mean, viz. *dôl* a meadow + *gwâr*, 'mild', 'gentle', 'pure', 'pleasant' (it appears to equate with *tirion* and other words more or less indicative of pleasantness) then it is a rather appropriate site-name for Ann's habitation, still more when the parish or locality chanced to be Llanfihangel-yng Ngwynfa, for is not *gwynfa one* of the Welsh terms for paradise? It merely struck me as a remarkable coincidence, – that's all, – that is, unless my etymology (a dangerous matter to meddle in, without proper foundation) is all astray. But it struck me that supposing we were dealing with some figure about whom legend had clustered who lived a millennium and a half back, in say the 'Age of the Saints' in 6th Cent. Wales, instead of a figure of only a century and a half back, then I can imagine the learned might well tend to suspect these site- and locality-names as – what's the term they use? – 'onomastic' (?) juggling by later hagiographical writers, 'In that dear middle-age these noodles praise', to accommodate the site-names with the character of the person associated with those sites.

David Jones's hesitation about the etymology of Dolwar is perhaps justified. It seems possible that the second syllable of the name comes from the word *gwar*, which means 'nape of the neck', and hence 'upper part' or 'verge', rather than from *gwâr*, pleasant. But *Gwynfa* surely means blessed place or paradise, and the name of the church to which Ann Griffiths went Sunday by Sunday in her youth is surely suggestive enough. A hilltop church of St Michael the Archangel is a suitable site for the baptism and burial of one who longed so ardently to share in the vision and the song of the angelic hosts.

The Mystery of the Incarnation; the Plygain *Carols and the work of Ann Griffiths*

To speak of the incarnation is to speak of the meeting of heaven and earth, of eternity and time, of God and man. It involves a bringing together of things small, intimate, touched and known, with things immense, transcendent, unimaginable and unknown. It means the coming together of the long slow processes of time with the sudden and unpredictable gifts of eternity. When we look in the Gospels at the accounts of Christ's birth we find that they tell us not only of a gift from above, but also of a long and painful human ancestry. The new man is rooted in history, in the particular history of his own people. The universal is made known in what is most limited and specific.

What is true of the one unique and all encompassing moment of the incarnation of the Word, is true of every lesser moment where something of eternity becomes embodied in the world of time. It is true in some measure of every human birth, for every human birth involves this meeting between the age-old processes of evolution and the radically new thing which comes into existence in the emergence of new possibilities of human freedom and creativity. Beyond this, every man or woman who has received some special gift of wisdom and insight, of utterance or song, is at once the product of their own time and place, and at the same time independent of it, rooted in one particular soil, yet growing beyond it into something larger and more universal, able to speak across the barriers of space and time.

This meeting of time and eternity in the life and utterance of a particular human being creates the fabric of human history, a pattern of timeless moments which occur when time touches what is beyond time. It creates too the fabric of human geography, a pattern of places which have been marked for ever by those who have lived in them. There is a particular mystery about the interpenetration of person and place which has been noticed in many different cultures. Places are marked by the people who live in them. People are formed by the places where they live. Who can doubt that our appreciation of the Lake District or the Wye valley is marked for ever by Wordsworth's visionary lines, lines which will live as long as the English language is alive and understood?

This interaction of people and place is something which has been felt particularly strongly amongst the Celtic people from the beginning of their history until today. One of the earliest Irish poems speaks of it.

> The fort in front of the oakwood
> belonged to Bruidge, and Cathal,
> belonged to Aedh, and Ailill,
> belonged to Conaing, and Culine,
> and to Mael Duin before them,
> – all kings in their turn.
> The fort survives; the kings
> are covered in clay.[1]

In our own century the Welsh philosopher, J. R. Jones, has written of this interpenetration, this *cydymdreiddiad*, with specially sharp emphasis, for where the existence of a language is threatened, there the whole memory of a people is in danger, and with it the very existence of the places where they live. The places of that people are no longer remembered, no longer known and loved.

This interpenetration of people and place takes a very special form in the case of those whose lives are shaped by the practice of prayer and praise. The places where such people live tend to become holy places which reveal the latent quality which is present in every place. The potential sacredness of every place is drawn out and made explicit by the holiness which such lives embody. And this quality shows itself to be remarkably resilient. It can persist across the centuries, even across centuries of forgetfulness and neglect. This is the secret of the ancient places of

pilgrimage in this island of Britain, many of which have come to
life again in this century against every expectation, against every
probability, Iona and Walsingham, Bardsey and Canterbury,
Glastonbury and Little Gidding. In such places we seem to have
access through the passage of time to an eternal reality beyond the
passage to time. In coming to such places, as Eliot says,

> You are not here to verify,
> Instruct yourself, or inform curiosity
> Or carry report. You are here to kneel
> Where prayer has been valid. And prayer is more
> Than an order of words, the conscious occupation
> Of the praying mind, or the sound of the voice praying.
> And what the dead had no speech for, when living,
> They can tell you, being dead; the communication
> Of the dead is tongued with fire beyond the language
>   of the living.[2]

In the holy places of our island the interpenetration of person
and place has created a sacred space in which time and eternity
can meet, a permanent place where men and women can find
healing and peace through the openness of our little world which
passes away to the great world which lasts for ever. Little Gidding
in England where Nicholas Ferrar lived, the place of which Eliot
sang, Dolwar Fach in Wales where Ann Griffiths passed the whole
of her brief life, celebrated in the lines of R. S. Thomas, are just
such places. Through such a life as hers Dolwar Fach is
inseparably united with the great resurrection.

This chapter looks a little more at the region to which it belongs
and examines one particular element in its tradition, an element
which helps us to appreciate better the wonder of the unity
between the particular and the universal which is set up through
her. For Ann was also a product of her own time and place, and if
she grew beyond it, none the less she was rooted in it.

I

Every part of our island has been given its own beauty. Of
nowhere is this more true than Wales which in a comparatively

small space encompasses a great variety of landscape and scenery. Maldwyn, Montgomeryshire, where Ann lived, is part of the ancient kingdom of Powys, *Powys paradwys Cymru*, (Powys, the paradise of Wales), as the old poets say, *Powys Paradwys brodyr*, (Powys, the paradise of brothers), the middle kingdom in the world of Wales between Gwynedd to the north and Deheubarth to the south, confronting England across the barrier of Offa's Dyke. In parts it is a very fertile, welcoming region; people speak of *mwynder* Maldwyn, the gentleness of Maldwyn. But in parts it can be wild and bare and rugged. Ann's parish lies between the two extremes, between the heights of the Berwyns on the one side, and the rich plains which stretch down into Shropshire on the other. It is a country of swift streams and steep hills. We hear an echo of it in her letters. 'I am sometimes out of breath on the slopes.'

R. S. Thomas who has lived and worked in that area speaks of it from inside knowledge.

> I know
> Powys, the leafy backwaters
> it is easy for the spirit to forget
> its destiny in and put on soil
> for its crown.

But that was not a trap which Ann was to fall into

> You walked solitary
> there and were not tempted
> or took your temptation as calling
> to see Christ rising in April
> out of that same soil and clothing
> his nakedness like a tree.

She may have been rooted in the earth, indeed she must have been, rooted in all the heavy and repetitious tasks of a working farm in days long before labour-saving devices had been thought of, but her mind and heart were open to heaven. As she hastened towards the great world which lasts for ever, she sometimes had a painful sense of the pressures of eternity on time, of the pressures of

divine judgement on us frail creatures of time and space. For her
there could be no final settling down into the sheltering routines of
domestic life. Yet it was in and through such prosaic things that
her gift was given.

If she was shaped by Dolwar Fach, her presence there has made
of that place a holy place for ever. As R. S. Thomas declares,

> Here for a few years
> the Spirit sang on a bare bough
> at eternity's window, the flesh trembling
> at the splendour of a forgiveness
> too impossible to believe in, yet believing.[3]

Ann Griffiths was rooted not only in the work of the farm, but in
the life of her parish. Her family was one which was devoted to the
church. Her father had been churchwarden there. Prayers from
the Book of Common Prayer were said in the family every day;
there were few who were more regular in church attendance at
Llanfihangel-yng-Ngwynfa than the Thomases of Dolwar Fach.
It is said that their old dog was so much in the habit of going to
church with them, that when the family deserted the church for
the Methodists, the dog would still go on his own.

The story of the Church of England in Wales in the seventeenth
and eighteenth centuries is not always a happy one. Especially in
the latter century, absentee English bishops, ill-educated and
poorly paid clergy, failures in teaching and preaching, were
unfortunately common. But the picture has been painted too
monotonously black. There were positive elements in the situation which have often been forgotten. One of these elements is to
be found in the carols associated with the early morning service on
Christmas day, called the *plygain*. One of the most dramatic events
in Ann's life is connected with the *plygain* of 1796, the moment
when she finally turned her back on the parish church. What was
this *plygain* which was such a feature of church life in Ann
Griffiths's day and which is still, in a slightly different form, a
feature of the life of that district today? Can it tell us something
about the background of her hymns, about the assumptions
which she and her neighbours would have made about them?

To explain the *plygain* we need to go far back into history, for we touch here a tradition which has its origins in the early Christian centuries.[4] The word has a Latin root. It comes from *galli cantus* or *pulli cantus*, words which mean *cock-crow* and which have come to signify the hour before dawn. In old Welsh usage the word *plygain* is often coupled with *gosber*; a pair equivalent to the English *mattins* and *evensong*. But the word also seems to have become particularly associated with the pre-Reformation dawn mass of Christmas, the mass at cock-crow, a service which in post-Reformation times was often transmuted into an early morning service of mattins. The earliest texts of *plygain* carols which we have date from the seventeenth century, and already we hear not only of extensive carol-singing in church, but also of extensive carol-singing through the hours of the night as groups of singers went from house to house on their way to church.

These *plygain* carols need to be seen in relation to other kinds of popular songs, sacred and secular, and in particular to two other kinds of carols which date from the same period or earlier, the *cwndidau* and *halsingod*. If *plygain* carols are typical of north and central Wales, *cwndidau* and *halsingod* seem to have flourished in the south. All these different kinds of carols have it in common that they were written not in the old strict metres of the bardic schools, but in the new free metres which became popular in the seventeenth century. These free metres were less complex than the metres of the Middle Ages, though some at least of the techniques of alliteration and assonance, *cynghanedd*, which had marked the older poetry of the bards were carried on in them. *Plygain* carols, *cwndidau* and *halsingod* were popular religious poems intended to be sung both at home and in church. They were written to highly singable tunes, and express the faith and vision of seventeenth-century Anglicanism.

But while the earliest texts for such carols for the most part date from that century, it seems probable that the tradition which they represent goes back a good deal further. Dr Rachel Bromwich is not alone in arguing that a long tradition of popular oral poetry lies behind the free-metre poetry which was first written down in the seventeenth century. The *cwndidau* indeed can be traced back to the fifteenth century, and the word *cwndid*, like *plygain*, has its origin in liturgical Latin. It comes from the Latin word *conductus*, the name for a chant sung as the priest was going up to the altar. It would seem that the *plygain* carols, even if in their present form they date from the seventeenth century, may well be heirs to older, pre-Reformation traditions of vernacular religious song.

In her study of the *plygain* carols Dr Enid Pierce Roberts points to five features which characterize them.[5] First, they are resolutely biblical in their contents and exclude non-biblical and legendary material. Here we see a clear indication of the influence of the Reformation. Secondly however, they are always written in the *we* form rather than the *I* form. They express corporate rather than individual devotion, and in that sense, though popular, they have a liturgical quality to them. Thirdly, while they dwell on the story of Christmas and the mystery of the incarnation, they by no means stop there. They look on to the whole story of Christ, not least to his suffering and death, to his resurrection and to his coming in glory. Fourthly, they often contain a strong element of moral exhortation. But this does not overshadow their fifth and final characteristic. They are above all songs of joyful celebration. God is perceived as generous and merciful, rather than as the God of wrath and judgement.

Cwndidau and *halsingod*, so far as I know, are things of the past. *Plygain* carols most certainly are not. It is true that, whereas in the nineteenth and early twentieth century *plygain* services seem to have taken place in many parts of Wales, now they are mainly to be found in one district of mid Wales, the Tanat valley area, the area where Ann lived. It is true too that they are no longer celebrated in the early morning, but usually in the evening in the weeks following Christmas. But this being said, the service itself, and the way in which it is conducted, seems to have remained remarkably stable during recent centuries. It begins, if it is celebrated in church, with a greatly shortened form of mattins or evensong. Then come the carols. They are sung by a variety of local groups, often quite small, consisting of three or four singers, for the most part unaccompanied and for a large part men. There is no announcer, and no previously worked-out programme. People feel instinctively when it is the right moment for their group to come out and sing, and the service may well last two hours or more.

Thus it is very much a service which belongs to the people. Particular groups of singers, often family groups, have their own special carols. Speaking of her memories of the *plygain* at Llanllyfni in Caernarfonshire early in this century, Ann Wood Griffiths recalls

> very happy times . . . when our fathers used to take their little 'corau aelwyd' (family choirs) right to the chancel to sing their carols. My father and Mr Jones, Shop yr Hall, Mr John Thomas, watchmaker . . . and all the other heads of families used to take part.

Songs which had been prepared and learnt at home were shared with the whole congregation. Here was an element in the folk tradition of pre-Methodist Wales of which Methodism did not disapprove. It was something which appealed to church and chapel people alike. Speaking of the same parish in the period before the First World War, a Methodist minister could write

> What a thrill it was to attend the parish church at Llanllyfni for the carol service at five o'clock in the morning! We tramped there together in crowds, all denominational pride gone and all arguments forgotten. Were we not on the way to Bethlehem? I remember the shadows lingering in the corners of the old church, and the sons of the sexton singing like the angels of God.[6]

One small detail about the way in which the *plygain* carols are sung today is particularly relevant to one of the salient facts which we know about Ann Griffiths and her hymns. The *plygain* singers like to sing by heart, and when they use a book they prefer to use a hand-written exercise book. The tradition is still basically an oral one, backed up by manuscript material, despite the fact that the texts which are sung have nearly all been printed at one time or another. Now one of the most striking facts about Ann for the twentieth-century reader is that she never made a fair copy of her hymns. Indeed often she seems not to have written them down at all. After composing them, she shared them with Ruth her companion, and it was Ruth who, being a good singer, provided the tunes to fit the words. It is through Ruth's dictation of the words to her husband, John Hughes, Pontrobert, after Ann's death, that Ann's texts are preserved for posterity. Seen against the background of the *plygain* tradition, this example of oral tradition at the beginning of the nineteenth century is less surprising than it might otherwise be.

II

But it is of course with the contents of the carols that we are most concerned. Do they in any way show the same interests, the same themes, the same methods as Ann's hymns? We must at the outset make it clear that Ann's hymns are *not* carols. For one thing, they are written in the first person singular and express the personal and fervent devotion which is characteristic of the Methodist movement, but is not at all typical of the *plygain* tradition. Again in Ann's hymns the use of *cynghanedd* is only occasional and almost accidental. Ann's verses are clearly Methodist hymns written under the influence of Pantycelyn and the other great hymn-writers of the first generation of the Methodist movement. But this being said, we may still ask whether it is not possible to see at least some traces of the influence of the *plygain* carols in Ann's hymns, for the carols were texts with which she must have been familiar from her childhood.

I would suggest that we can see at least three major signs of such influence. First there is the very full use of the Old Testament images and types to speak of Christ. Ann sees Christ everywhere in the pages of the Old Testament. So do the carol writers. So in one carol we sing,

On this day's morn, a little child, a little child,
The root of Jesse was born, a little child,
The Mighty One of Bozra,
The Lawgiver on Mount Sinai,
The Atonement won on Calvary, a little child, a little child,
Sucking at Mary's breast, a little child.

The living waters of Ezekiel, on Mary's knee, on Mary's
    knee.

The Daniel's true Messiah on Mary's knee,
The wise child of Isaiah,
The promise given to Adam,
The Alpha and Omega, on Mary's knee, on Mary's knee,
In a stall in Bethlehem Judah, on Mary's knee.[7]

Closely related to this first point is a second one. This is the
elaborate and delighted use of paradoxes to express the wonder of
the incarnation. This is of course part of the stock in trade of
Christian faith and poetry through the ages, but it is present to a
special degree in Ann's hymns, and it is no less present in the carols
of the *plygain* tradition. I take a text which dates from the middle
of the nineteenth century, well after Ann's time, but which seems
to be typical of the earlier tradition as well.

Look around us, who created these
Sun, moon, stars and the earth which smiles so fair?
They whirl through space, held there by his word
While he leans on Mary's gentle breast.

The boy who was born, but a span's length at birth
Is the Son whose span measures the whole world,
A tiny babe on his mother's breast
And yet able to support the whole universe safely.[8]

Another text which comes from the sexton of the parish church at
Llanllyfini (Robert Ellis, 1829–72) of which we have already
heard, uses other images to make the same point.

The great infinite being
Sustainer of the mighty worlds
A smiling gracious rose
On the Virgin Mary's knee.[9]

In this case it is interesting to note the same word Sustainer,
Cynhaliwr, that we find in one of the greatest of Ann's verses.

Wonderful, wonderful in the sight of angels
A great wonder in the eyes of faith,
To see the giver of being, the generous sustainer

And ruler of all things
In the manger, in swaddling clothes
And without a place to lay his head
And yet the bright hosts of glory worshipping him now.

In the *plygain* carols the images which are all, or nearly all,
taken from the Bible are often combined in original and
sometimes startling ways. So a later verse from the first carol
which we quoted, runs as follows

Righteousness was satisfied, through the work of the
Atonement
And the law was held in honour, through the work of
the Atonement.
Great hell is shaking
The turtle dove is singing,
And God and man are smiling, through the work of the
Atonement
In peace in the person of Jesus, through the work of the
Atonement.

In a carol which is today often sung at the end of the *plygain*,
there is an exhortation to the congregation to hasten to enter into
the covenant which God offers us in his Son. Here the images of
the nails of the cross, of the heavenly feast, of the return of the
prodigal are combined in a very striking way. This again is part of
the backcloth against which we need to see Ann's hymns.

Today is the day of the covenant, and the supper is ready
With the table laid, O, let us hurry!
The hands that were nailed are welcoming prodigal
children
Into the land of the heavenly Canaan to feast for ever.
Amen, Amen; praise be for ever. Amen.
Halleluia to the Messiah who always forgives. Amen.[10]

In his introduction to the book, *Homage to Ann Griffiths*,
published in 1976, the bicentenary year of her birth, H. A.
Hodges wrote,

One feature of Ann's literary style which is often remarked upon is the richness and boldness of her imagery. The principal and almost sole source from which she draws it is the Bible, and in that she does not differ from the general run of devout writers in the tradition to which she belongs. What is outstanding in her work is the richness of the texture into which she weaves this material. It is safe to say that the reader of Ann who is not familiar with the text of Scripture, not just its general drift, but its actual words and phrases will constantly fail to see her point.[11]

The 'carpenters of song' who composed the *plygain* carols do not generally have Ann's peculiar genius. but they too are sometimes rich and bold in their use of biblical imagery.

In general, as has been said, the tone of the carols is objective, and their method historical, tracing Christ's journey from Bethlehem to the cross, from the empty tomb to the moment of ascension. Their versification is by no means always accomplished or polished. They can become prosaic and moralizing. Yet there are moments in the carols when they surprise us by their theological and spiritual insight, moments when they seem to rise beyond themselves into a quality of wisdom and a depth of feeling which we hardly expected. Here is the third point where they may directly remind us of Ann.

For Ann, the salvation of humankind consists in being drawn into the very life of the Triune God. We are from all eternity objects of the primal love. In the counsel of the Three in One the salvation of humankind has been planned since before the foundation of the world. Already now we can at least taste that fullness of life which shall be ours in the kingdom, already now we can enter into 'the dwelling places of the Three in One'. Such a vision is not common; certainly we do not often find it in the *plygain* carols. But consider the following verses.

> Our great king and brother came
> Clothed in created flesh
> Wonderful was the sight of the son of the Lord God
> At the breast of the sweet Virgin
> This wonder will not cease for all eternity.

O, may the Comforter give wings to every talent
To sing our happiness and joy.
A plygain song of an historical nature
Is not sufficient rejoicing for the believing soul
But only to see the chosen divine face of Jesus.

An order was opened through freely granted love
Flowing outward like a fountain
Of grace, with its gifts for the race of mankind
From the bosom of God himself.
Through the Three in One it was ordained
That there must be shedding of blood
To spare the dust of earth's wretches . . . [12]

It is in the counsel of the Three in One that an order was ordained
for the salvation of man. This order, what in the language of
patristic theology is called the divine economy, flows out from the
fountain of self-giving love which is at the very heart of the
Godhead. The incarnation of the Word, the sacrificial death on
the cross, these are things seen from all eternity. They are
expressions of the love of the Trinity. In a carol which we have
quoted before, we sing

Let us consider the love of the Trinity, freely willed, freely
willed
In setting out a way of covenant, freely willed
The Father chose the surety,
The Son was content to suffer
The Holy Spirit gave his gifts, freely willed, freely willed
To bring Zion home, freely willed.

III

It is the salvation of Zion, not just of the individual which has been
freely willed from all eternity. We find this vision in the Welsh
Methodist hymn writers. We find it in the *plygain* carols too. The
verse which speaks of the inadequacy of a historical *plygain* song to
express the joy of the believer comes from the pen of David
Thomas (Dafydd Ddu Eryri, 1759–1822) an older contemporary
of Ann's, and was published in a collection which saw the light of

day in 1810.[13] It was the work of a man who was a weaver's son and who later became a schoolmaster. Like Ann, his formal schooling was of the slightest, but this did not prevent him from becoming a master of the classical arts of bardic poetry, at a time when such experts were very few. In the latter years of the eighteenth century he gathered a group of younger poets around him and had a considerable influence on their development. The carol from which we have quoted is written in the seventeenth-century free-metre style, but with full use of *cynghanedd*. Both in its form and its content it bears witness to the extraordinary continuity of tradition which marks the poetic activities of the Celtic countries. It speaks of a popular tradition which yet conserves something of the skill and articulation of an earlier, more professional and aristocratic literary period. It is the product of a man who was an accomplished poet, and who, without being a theologian in the academic sense of that word, is very evidently a theologian in the older sense, one who sees deeply into the things of God and declares what he sees. He is surely a witness not only to a poetic tradition, but to the tradition of the church. Thus we can find at the end of the eighteenth century unsuspected resources of insight and understanding, and an unlooked for and almost unconscious continuity of the tradition of faith and praise across the discontinuities of church history.

A similar interaction of poetic and religious insights is to be seen in the writing of the one real scholar to be found in the circle in which Ann moved. Thomas Jones of Denbigh (1756–1820) was the outstanding intellectual figure in the Calvinistic Methodism of north Wales during this period. In many ways Thomas Jones is a typical Evangelical of the early nineteenth century. In some ways, he is not. As we have already seen, through the Welsh poetic tradition he had direct access to elements in the Christian understanding of the world which would not have been open in the same way to his contemporaries in England or America. The Evangelical emphasis on redemption and on atonement is balanced and completed by the earlier Catholic emphasis on creation, and by the vision of the world and everything in it as sacramental. This is the milieu in which Ann was living. This is the milieu in which past and present, popular and professional, feeling and thinking could come together in ways which surprise and amaze us.

Ann had received in her parish and in her home, not only the texts of the Bible and the Book of Common Prayer, but also a living tradition of sacred song, of various kinds of carols, popular and poetic, deeply felt yet strongly doctrinal, through which something of the poetic and theological vision of earlier centuries was preserved and maintained. The sacramental method of bardic verse was still being used in the service of the great paradoxes of the faith as it had been centuries before. The carols, unconsciously perhaps, conveyed a great wealth of inherited wisdom and insight. The devotion of the Middle Ages, the biblical learning of the Reformation period, the poetic techniques of the seventeenth century, the warmth of feeling of the common people of Wales, all these things had gone into their making, and had received new fire from the enthusiasm of Methodism. All this is part of what is behind Ann's hymns, part of what made their miracle possible. We begin to see a little more of the way in which, both in their form and in their content they speak to us of the mystery of the incarnation, the sudden unforeseeable gift prepared for by the slow processes of history.

If this is indeed the case, then it must follow that the tradition which speaks to us in Ann is of greater significance to us today than is commonly recognized. The memory of God and of the things of God which is embodied, incarnate in the language and literature of Wales, is of a particular quality; it is other than and in some respects richer than that which is accessible to us in English. It bears its own irreplaceable witness to the miracle of Emmanuel, God with us. We neglect it to our own great loss and peril. Its discovery or rediscovery is a matter of urgent importance, not only for Wales but for Britain as a whole. It has much to say to us about the potential which is hidden at the heart of every human life, about the possibility that here and now God may be known and loved in circumstances which appear outwardly poor and unpromising. It speaks of a vision both corporate and personal, of a historical tradition constantly renewed in the experience of successive generations, of the unbelievable fulfilment which our human existence can find in the coming of the Incarnate Word, in the presence of the Holy Spirit with his gifts.

The places which have been made holy in the growth of that tradition remain holy places. We may think specifically of the places touched for ever by the mystery of Ann's life and song, the old chapel at Pontrobert, the house at Dolwar Fach, the church at Llanfihangel-yng-Ngwynfa where she lies buried. These are places where Christian people of all traditions may be united in common acts of praise and thanksgiving, places whose holiness demands to be recognized more widely than it has been up till now.[14] There are possibilities of pilgrimage here which need to be explored in a variety of ways. Ann herself, surely, must become more consciously part of the memory of the people of Wales, whether Welsh- or English-speaking, and then of the people of Britain as a whole. Has not the time come when there should be some act of public recognition of her life on the part of all the churches in Wales? In the Church in Wales this could perhaps take the form of the inclusion of her name in the Prayer Book calendar. For here was one in whom the power of God was present and made known, one whose message has not ceased to sound across the centuries.

It sometimes seems as if the great figures of the church's history wrote and spoke for later ages than for their own. 'The communication of the dead is tongued with fire beyond the language of the living.' May we not find this to be the case with Ann, as we listen again to what she has to tell us, by her life and by her song, of the way in which God comes to meet us where we are in the midst of all the frailties and confusions, the limitations and blindness which mark our life in space and time?

Beauty will save the World: from Solzhenitsyn to Pantycelyn

At the beginning of the lecture in which he accepted the Nobel Prize for Literature, Solzhenitsyn quoted Dostoevsky's enigmatic remark, 'Beauty will save the world', and commented,

> What is this? For a long time it seemed to me simply a phrase. How could this be possible? When in the blood-thirsty process of history did beauty ever save anyone, and from what? Granted it enobled, it elevated — but who did it save?[1]

And yet, as he goes on at once to confess, there is in beauty a self-authenticating quality, a power of affirmation and attraction, which cannot be denied. While goodness and truth can be manipulated and used for purposes other than their own, beauty remains sovereign, elusive, unpredictable, free. Beauty indeed can never be a substitute for truth and goodness, but it may prove to be an indispensable complement to them. 'So perhaps the old trinity of Truth, Goodness and Beauty is not simply the decorous and antiquated formula' we have sometimes thought it to be. When the branches of truth and goodness are lopped and broken from the tree of life, 'the unpredictable and ever surprising shoots of Beauty force their way through' and soar up to crown and complete the tree.[2]

It is and it was a remarkable affirmation coming from a writer who has suffered and seen much, a writer whose basic moral options and perceptions we should not lose sight of in our possible impatience with the limitations of some of his more recent attitudes and judgements. It is an affirmation which makes very high claims for the artist. It declares that art has an essential part to play in saving humankind, in assuring the continuing identity of man as a creature who can know and love what is good, what is true, what is beautiful, and whose being can only find its fulfilment when that love and knowledge are fused together into a single movement of celebration and delight.

It is however not an affirmation which has claimed a very large place in the theological writing of the last two centuries. The saving power of beauty is not a subject treated in most textbooks of dogmatics. Theological reflection on man's relationship with God as the source of his identity and being has concentrated on the ethical and philosophical realms, not on the aesthetic. The theme of the beauty of God has not been greatly cultivated. It was not always so. Even at the end of the eighteenth century when a monastic scholar in Greece put together and published a great anthology of the spiritual and theological texts of the Eastern Church, a collection which was intended to recapitulate and resume a whole tradition, he called it the *Philokalia*, the love of the divine beauty, not the love of wisdom or the love of goodness. It was an anthology by no means unknown in the Russia of Dostoevsky.[3]

Furthermore, this neglected theme constitutes the heart of one of the most remarkable theological enterprises of the latter part of the twentieth century, a work which is now becoming available to us in English translation. I refer to Hans Urs von Balthasar's great *summa*, *Herrlichkeit*, or in English *The Glory of the Lord*. The work's subtitle is *A Theological Aesthetics*, not, be it noted, an aesthetic theology, a discussion of the nature of God carried on in terms of some general theory of beauty, but a theological aesthetics, an intense and systematic reflection on man's capacity to perceive, to see, to know the splendour which is in the world, and through and beyond it to come to know the splendour of the divine. In this process, von Balthasar is convinced,

> Beauty will not allow herself to be separated and banned from her two sisters, without taking them along with herself in an act of mysterious vengeance.

Without the recognition of the beauty which is in things, our perceptions of goodness decline into a mere moralism.

The good loses its attractiveness, the self-evidence of why it must be carried out. Man stands before the good and asks himself *why* it must be done, and not rather its alternative evil . . .

Similarly our perceptions of truth are reduced to the level of mere ideology.

Syllogisms may still dutifully spew out an exact number of answers by the minute. But the logic of these answers is itself a mechanism which no longer captivates anyone. The very conclusions are no longer conclusive.[4]

So von Balthasar embarks on his great undertaking, a sustained and calculated effort to reinstate the category of beauty in our approach to the divine. To see afresh the meaning of such words as 'grace' and 'glory'. The first volume of his work has as its subtitle *Schau der Gestalt* (*Seeing the Form*), an investigation of man's capacity to perceive the splendour of the form of things, to see this world as the creation of God and to perceive God himself in and through the things that he has made. It is a work which links the study of theology with the study of spirituality, the analytical with the experiential approach to the things of God. The witness of the men and women of prayer is given a primary place in it. The witness of the singing and praying congregation is scarcely less important. The frontiers between the study of theology and liturgy and the study of literature are opened up. So in the second and third volumes which contain a series of studies of outstanding figures in the development of the Christian tradition, the poets are there no less than those we are usually accustomed to call theologians, Dante, Gerard Manley Hopkins, Peguy, no less than Irenaeus, Gregory of Nyssa, Augustine. In this way von Balthasar's great work which began to see the light of day in Germany some twenty years ago proves to be highly relevant to some of the most urgent current concerns in the English-speaking theological world, in particular the steadily growing interest in the relation between faith and imagination, between theology and literature, and the new concern for the study of spirituality.

As von Balthasar's argument develops it becomes clear that the particular experience of the contemplatives, those who are often called mystics, is of vital importance to him. They are those who find themselves drawn out of themselves by the attractive power of a divine beauty, drawn out of themselves in a movement which involves both love and knowledge and which leads them towards an actual share in the being of the object of their contemplation. Saunders Lewis puts this with characteristic clarity in his classical essay on Ann Griffiths, speaking about the vision of the angelic hosts as,

> a selfless vision, a vision wholly appreciative, a vision full of wonder and worship and blessing and pure joy, without anything of self or any thought of self coming into it.

> (edrych anhunanol, hollol werthfawrogol, edrych sy'n rhyfeddu ac yn addoli ac yn fendithio, ac yn llawenydd pur, heb ddim o'r hunan, na chofio am hunan yn agos ato.)[5]

In this act of seeing, gazing, looking, with which the contemplative is associated so that it becomes both human and angelic, what we usually call subjective is linked with what we usually call objective. It is at once an intensely intimate inner experience, and yet it carries us out beyond ourselves in a movement involving our whole being, mind and feeling, emotion and will, body and spirit, a movement which takes us through the things of time into a realm beyond the reach of time.

The experience is, von Balthasar would maintain, something universal, part of what constitutes our common humanity, our capacity to perceive and recognize the beauty which is latent in the world, waiting to disclose itself. In the Christian tradition, this experience finds its culminating point in the person of Christ in whom the divine glory shines out, above all in the mystery of the cross, with such power as to create within us a capacity to respond which we did not even know we possessed. And at this point we see something of the strangeness, the paradoxical character of the divine beauty, for the man on the cross, is one 'without form or comeliness'. He makes himself known in the total offering of himself in love. God comes out of himself in a movement of *ecstatic* love for mankind and all creation, and in doing so draws man out of himself in a corresponding movement of return. This reciprocated movement is beautifully described by Pantycelyn in an English letter, where for a moment in English prose we catch a glimpse of the concise and epigrammatic clarity of his Welsh.

> A sight of his love is the cause of our love; and our thirst after him is but the effect of his thirst after us; and our diligence in seeking of him is the effect of his diligence in seeking of us.[6]

In more technical language von Balthasar sums up the matter thus,

> The object with which we are concerned is man's participation in God, which from God's perspective is actualised as 'revelation' (culminating in Christ's Godmanhood), and which from man's perspective is actualised as 'faith' (culminating in participation in Christ's Godmanhood). This double and reciprocal *ecstasis* – God's venturing forth to man, and man's to God – constitutes the very content of dogmatics, which may thus rightly be presented as a theory of rapture; the *admirabile commercium et connubium* between God and man in Christ as Head and Body.[7]

It will have become evident from even so brief an outline of the thesis of von Balthasar that this understanding of theology which places the mystical experience of exchange at its heart is one which is particularly congenial to the Catholicism of the Christian west and to the Orthodoxy of the Christian east. Its typical figures are a Symeon, the New Theologian in eleventh-century Constantinople, or a John of Cross in sixteenth-century Spain. But does it have any place within the world of the Reformation? Von Balthasar seems to say little if any. The theme of God as beauty, a beauty so compelling as to draw man out of himself into union with the divine, is, he maintains, one which in its traditional form has been repudiated in the world of the Reformation. 'Contemporary Protestant theology nowhere deals with the beautiful as a theological category.'[8]

I do not intend to take issue with von Balthasar directly on this matter. It is true that very little is said about beauty in twentieth-century Protestant theology, but I suspect that the theme of God as beauty was more present in the theological and spiritual world of continental Protestantism, at least in its first two centuries, than von Balthasar allows. Wherever *The Song of Songs* remains part of the canon of Scripture, and wherever its traditional interpretation in terms of the love of God for his creation is maintained, there this theme of the divine beauty is always liable to reassert itself. But as regards the Reformation traditions in this island, I am sure that von Balthasar is wrong. The vision of God's glory as a vision of beauty as well as of goodness and truth is powerfully present in some of their most classical representatives. To two of them, one English and one Welsh, I now intend to turn.

I

Richard Hooker (1554–1600) is without question the greatest systematic theologian of the sixteenth century in England. He is the man who above all others has left his mark on the subsequent development of Anglican theology, a man moreover whose authority is recognized by all the varying schools of thought within Anglicanism. Hooker's great work, *On the Laws of Ecclesiastical Polity*, was occasioned by certain sixteenth-century controversies about church order and forms of worship. But Hooker was a man who always liked to trace a problem back to the first principles which lie behind it. So his work is by no means exhausted by the questions with which it begins. It contains a profound treatment of the major strands of Christian reflection and not least a remarkable vision of the nature of man. In face of any tendency to denigrate humanity before God, to belittle the creature in order to exalt the Creator, Hooker stands for a theocentric vision of the glory of man, a creature who carries God's image and likeness within him. Human nature has at its heart a capacity to go beyond itself, an aptitude to be carried out beyond itself into a participation in the divine. Humankind is made by God in the beginning, is made for God in the end. Mortal, finite, fragile, our nature is yet open to receive what is immortal and eternal. All our powers of love and knowledge, of action and of suffering have their final fulfilment in God alone.[9]

> Complete union with him must be according unto every power and faculty of our minds apt to receive so glorious an object. Capable we are of God both by understanding and will: by understanding, as he is that saving Truth which comprehendeth the rich treasures of all wisdom; by will, as he is that sea of Goodness whereof whoso tasteth shall thirst no more. As the will doth now work upon that object by desire, which is as it were a motion towards the end as yet unobtained, so likewise upon the same hereafter received it shall work by love. *Appetitus inhiantis fit amor fruentis*, saith St Augustine: 'The longing disposition of them that thirst is changed into the sweet affection of them that taste and are replenished.' Whereas we now love that thing that is good, but good especially in respect of benefit unto us; we shall then love the thing that is good, only or principally, for the goodness of beauty itself. The soul being in this sort, as it is active, perfected by love of that infinite good, shall, as it is receptive, be also perfected with those supernatural passions of joy, peace and delight. All this endless and everlasting.[10]

This longing for what is infinite and eternal is seen by Hooker as something which affects men and women at every turn. There is a restlessness in human nature which manifests itself in a great variety of ways, an impulse which never rests satisfied with anything less than some ultimate fulfilment. But this longing in humanity for what is beyond us is constantly baffled. Our situation here in a world of finitude, imperfection, sin and death does not of itself open the way forward, the way which leads into that land which the heart and mind surmise rather than conceive, feel after without being able to attain.

The fulfilment we seek lies beyond us. The way towards it is opened up for us by a God who comes out from himself to meet us, and himself becomes the way along which we can pass into the fulfilment of his kingdom. Along that way we are guided by the three virtues, or powers, of faith, hope and love. Hooker takes up that classical Christian formulation, rooted of course in St Paul's first letter to the Corinthians, and develops the question in the following terms.

> Concerning Faith, the principal object whereof is that eternal Verity which hath discovered the treasures of hidden wisdom in Christ; concerning Hope, the highest object whereof is that everlasting Goodness which in Christ doth quicken the dead; concerning Charity, the final object whereof is that incomprehensible Beauty which shineth in the countenance of Christ the Son of the Living God; concerning these virtues, the first of which beginning here with a real apprehension of things not seen, endeth with the intuitive vision of God in the world to come; the second beginning here with a trembling expectation of things far removed and as yet only heard of, endeth with real and actual fruition of that which no tongue can express; the third beginning here with a weak inclination of heart towards him unto whom we are not able to approach endeth with endless union, the mystery whereof is higher than the reach of the thoughts of man . . . [11]

We notice at once that these three virtues which are all aspects of the one way which leads from earth to heaven, from time to eternity, from man to God, correspond in Hooker's thought to the three divine attributes of truth, goodness and beauty. Man puts his faith, his trust in God's truth, God's faithfulness, and so grows gradually to be faithful and true in himself. Man puts his hope, his expectation in God's creative and redeeming goodness, and so comes himself to share in something of God's eternal newness of life. But man's love, which in the end becomes a selfless love, a love wholly appreciative, a love full of wonder and worship and blessing and pure joy, is always response. It is something which must be captured and empowered by the divine beauty, the splendour of God's majesty, the strength of his mercy which is nowhere more fully revealed than in 'his tender compassion rescuing us drowned and swallowed up in misery'.[12] Not only are the three attributes of God, the three sisters as von Balthasar calls them, seen dancing together here in perfect harmony; it is beauty who is the leader of the dance. In heaven man indeed shares in the worship of the angels, of whom Hooker says, beholding the face of God, in admiration of so great excellency they all adore him, and being rapt with the love of his beauty, they cleave inseparably for ever unto him.[13]

Von Balthasar remarks in one place, 'a theology of beauty may be elaborated only in a beautiful manner',[14] and speaking of Richard Hooker in the appropriate volume of the *Oxford History of English Literature*, C. S. Lewis declares 'the style is for its purpose, perhaps the most perfect in English'.[15] Although there were many Anglican theologians in the seventeenth century who were to speak of God as beauty, none did so more beautifully than Hooker had done.

II

We turn now from sixteenth-century England to eighteenth-century Wales, to look at another classical figure in the Christian tradition of our island, another passionate singer of the divine beauty, William Williams, Pantycelyn (1717–91).

> Bydd dy degwch fyth yn newydd,
>   Fyth o newydd ennyn dân
> Trwy holl oesoedd tragwyddoldeb
>   Fyth heb flino yn y blaen;
> Fflam angerddol, heb un terfyn,
>   Trwy holl raddau'r nef yn un,
> Hi barhau i losgi'n olau
>   Tra parhao Duw ei Hun.[16]

(Thy beauty will be for ever new, ever freshly kindling a fire, through all the ages of eternity, evermore without failing; a fervent flame without end, through all the degrees of heaven together, it will continue to burn brightly as long as God himself shall last.)

We could spend a long time discussing the question whether Pantycelyn may rightly be seen as a representative of the same tradition as Richard Hooker. But this is not the occasion to do it. I would wish simply to state the conviction, that while we are doubtless right to acknowledge all that Welsh Methodism owes to the Puritans, as Dr Glyn Tegai Hughes for instance does in his study of Pantycelyn,[17] we should not overlook the extent to which the three great leaders of the movement in Wales were conscious of their roots in the tradition of the Church of England, and through it of their share in a larger, older, more universal inheritance of faith and life. Considering how little understanding they received from the bishops of their time it is remarkable to see that in their own way the Methodist leaders in Wales were as reluctant as the Wesleys in England to make a definitive break with the Established Church. Think for a moment of the terms in which at the end of his life Pantycelyn wrote to Thomas Charles. In his letter of 25 May 1790, a kind of testament of faith, he warns against errors in 'life doctrine and behaviour'. In life, he says, there are dangers of 'lukewarmness, indifference and idleness' on the one hand, and of 'bigotry, enthusiasm and party zeal on the other'. In behaviour he sees temptations either to lack of discipline and irregularity on the one side, or to pride, self-conceit and even heresy on the other. And then he goes on,

> Know my dear brother that heresies now as in the apostles' time are conceived and brought forth amongst many sects and denominations of people and boldly preached out without shame or detraction, but as Methodism so far has been kept clear from the so pernicious and destructive tares, I hope the Lord will preserve us to the end — as we have continued now near 60 years orthodox in the faith, I doubt not but we shall spend out our century without erring either in life or doctrine — the articles of the Church of England, the Nicean and Athanasian Creeds, the lesser and larger catechism of the assembly with their confession of faith are some of the grandest and most illustrious beauties of the Reformation.[18]

While we may smile at the inclusion of the Nicene and Athanasian creeds among the beauties of the Reformation, nothing could be clearer than Pantycelyn's desire first to avoid all forms of sectarianism, and then to affirm his adherence to that common inheritance of faith which the Reformers had carried

over from the early centuries of the church, and in particular to
their affirmation of the central doctrines of the Trinity and the
incarnation. Just as in the tradition which von Balthasar
represents, so here in Pantycelyn, the doctrines of the Trinity
and the incarnation are seen not as abstract, metaphysical
speculations, but as ways of expressing and safeguarding the heart
of Christian faith and experience, that astonishing sense of the
nearness and intimacy of God and man in Christ which lies at the
heart of the Methodist movement.[19] Here, as there, the wonderful
exchange and marriage of human and divine in Christ Jesus is
celebrated and affirmed. Threats to these inner-most structures of
Christian faith and thought are seen as threats to the very
possibility of growth in Christian life and prayer, personal and
corporate.

Thus it becomes more and more evident that for it to be fully
understood we need to see Pantycelyn's teaching in relation to this
whole inheritance of faith and theology. The structures of his
theological thought go back not only to the Reformation, but
before the Reformation. As Dr R. Tudur Jones has pointed out, for
instance, his understanding of the effects of sin can be paralleled in
the thought of Thomas Aquinas, his vision of the triumph of the
cross can be seen as rooted in the patristic understanding of Christ
as the conqueror of death and hell.[20] The classical doctrine of the
incarnation lies at the foundation of all his teaching. Among all the
wonders of heaven, he tells us, the greatest is to see the infinite,
divine being, clothed with the nature of man. It is this mystery
which reveals to him as to Hooker, the true and unsuspected
capacity of our human nature, made by God in the beginning,
made for God in the end. For him, as for the contemplative saints of
previous ages, the vision of heaven is a vision of the divine beauty, a
vision which draws man out of himself, transforming him into the
likeness of him in whose image he is made. Again it is a vision in
which love and knowledge are both involved, fused together into
one, into a movement which while it begins here has its fulfilment
beyond this world of space and time.

> Os yw tegwch d'wyneb yma
> Yn rhoi myrdd i'th garu'n awr,

Beth a wna dy degwch hyfryd
  Yna'n nhragwyddoldeb mawr?
    Nef y nefoedd
    A'th ryfedda fyth heb drai.

Pa fath uchder fydd i'm cariad,
  Pa fath syndod y pryd hyn,
Pryd y gwelwyf dy ogoniant
  Perffaith llawn ar Seion fryn?
    Anfeidroldeb
    O bob tegwch maith yn un.

Pa feddyliau uwch eu deall
  A gaf ynof fi fy hun,
Wrth ystyried bod y Duwdod
  Perffaith pur a minnau'n un?
    Dyma gwlwm
    Nad oes iaith a'i dyd i maes.

Cwlwm wnaed yn nhragwyddoldeb,
  Sicir, cadarn, mawr ei rym;
Ni all myrddiwn o flynddoedd
  Dorri hwn, na'i ddatod ddim:
    Gwna, fe bery
    Tra parhao Duw mewn bod.[21]

(If here the beauty of thy face makes myriads love thee now, what will thy glad beauty do yonder in eternity? The heavens will marvel at thee ceaselessly for ever. What height will my love reach, what wonder then, when I shall see thy full perfect glory on Mount Zion? Infinity of the whole range of beauties in one! What thoughts above understanding shall I have within me when I consider that the perfect pure Godhead and I are one? Here is a bond which there is no language to express. A bond that was made in eternity, sure, strong, very powerful; a myriad years cannot break it or undo it at all: it abides and will abide while God remains in being.)

The opening verse here speaks of the tension between what is known now, partially and in fragments, and that fullness of vision which belongs to eternity. The two following verses speak of the heights and depths which first love and then knowledge will attain there in the vision of eternity. It is interesting to notice that, as in Hooker, it is love which perceives God's glory as beauty, as the infinity of all beauties gathered into one, while faith is carried out of itself into a knowledge which is beyond knowledge, the knowledge that the perfect pure Godhead and I are one. This is a unity which is based in and follows directly from the unity of God and man in Jesus Christ. This unity of human and divine is a bond made from all eternity which no power in heaven or on earth can break.

Here we come to one of the favourite subjects of meditation in the whole of Welsh Methodism, the bond between man and God made in Christ from all eternity. Before creation, before the fall, there is a covenant bond rooted in the very being of God as love, in the eternal love which unites the three persons of the Trinity in the mystery of their divine being. 'The Fellowship in God the source of humanity's fellowship with God,' as an Anglican preacher of the nineteenth century put it.[22] The doctrine of the Trinity and the doctrine of the Incarnation are inseparably united.

> Cyn llunio'r byd, cyn lledu'r nefoedd wen,
> Cyn gosod haul, na lloer, na sêr uwchben,
> Fe drefnwyd ffordd yng nghyngor Tri yn Un
> I achub gwael golledig euog ddyn.[23]

(Before the world was made, before the bright heavens were stretched out, before the sun or the moon or the stars were set above, a way was set forth in the council of the Three in One, to save poor, lost, guilty man.)

This thought about the Council of the Three in One, the conviction that man's salvation is rooted in the very heart of God, this belief that we are loved with an everlasting love, found visual expression in another part of the Christian world, geographically far removed from Wales. There it gave birth to one of the most perfect, painted expressions of Christian faith in the whole of the Church's history. This is the icon of the Holy Trinity painted in Russia in the fourteenth century by the monk St Andrey Rublyov himself a disciple of the Abbot Sergius of Radonezh one of the great figures in Russian history, and founder of the monastery of the Holy Trinity at Zagorsk, which has remained through all the changes following 1917, a living centre of faith and pilgrimage. It is a striking fact that in the Council held in Moscow in June 1988, the Russian Orthodox Church decided to canonize Andrey Rublyov thus affirming again the transcendent value of his work.

In Eastern Orthodoxy, which has thought more about the nature of visual images than western Christendom, any direct representation of God the Father is forbidden. Rublyov's Trinity is an indirect, symbolic representation of the Godhead. It is based on an incident in the Old Testament. Three angels come to visit Abraham as he sits at the door of his tent in the heat of the day under the oaks of Mamre. The angels accept the hospitality of Abraham and Sarah. In this particular icon, the result of a long process of experimentation and simplification in the depiction of the scene, we see only the three angels seated around a table on which there stands a single dish. The eternal rather than the temporal meaning of the scene is emphasized. The angels are depicted in a serene conversation. They form a circle around the table, turning to one another. But it is an open circle. We are not excluded. The whole atmosphere of the icon is one of peace and luminous presence. It is

> Ffynhonnell y cariad tragwyddol
> Hen gartref meddyliau o hedd.[24]

(Fountain of eternal love, ancient dwelling place of thoughts of peace.)

But at the centre of the table there stands a dish with a slain lamb on it. From a purely visual point of view it looks like a wound in the middle of the composition. It tells us that sacrificial, self-giving love is at the heart of the Godhead. It speaks to us about the altar of sacrifice which stands at the heart of Christian worship. Moreover a careful analysis of the visual structure of the icon shows that hidden in the composition of the picture there is both a circle and a cross. The eternal covenant of love made in the being of God from all eternity finds its fullest expression in space and time in the utter self-giving of Calvary. As a contemporary Russian theologian puts it, 'The incarnation is the projection of the sacrificial love at the heart of the Trinity into the life of the cosmos and of humanity'.[25]

It is this love of which the verse of Hugh Derfel Hughes, from which I have just quoted, speaks,

> Y gŵr a fu gynt o dan hoelion
> Dros ddyn pechadurus fel fi,
> A yfodd y Cwpan i'r gwaelod
> Ei hunan ar ben Calfari
>
> Ffynhonnell y cariad tragwyddol
> Hen gartref meddyliau o hedd
> Dwg finnau i'r unrhyw gyfamod,
> Na thorrir gan angau, na'r bedd.[26]

(The man who was nailed to the cross, for a sinful man like me, drank the cup to the dregs, he himself on Calvary Hill; fountain of eternal love, ancient dwelling place of thoughts of peace, lead me to a covenant which neither death nor the grave can break.)

The serene beauty of the icon is not the product of an age which was untroubled by war, famine, violence and cruelty. It was painted by a man who lived by the cross of the monastic life. Whatever we may make of the sometimes puzzling detail of the film on Andrey Rublyov made some years ago in Soviet Russia by the famous director Tarkovsky, this much is clear. The film intends to show us that works full of such peace can come out of a world as violent and perplexing as our own. Such icons as those of Rublyov bring something of the divine peace and strength into such a world. They reveal the beauty of a divine compassion which shines out in the luminous colours as well as in the symbolic forms. They are works which are wholly rooted in the victory of the cross. Faced with them we begin to see more of why it should be in the Russian tradition that it can be said, 'Beauty will save the world'. Standing before this presence of the Trinity we may well reflect on some words of Pantycelyn in a quieter, less exultant mood.

Nac aed o'th gof dy ffyddlon amod drud,
Yn sicir wnaed cyn rhoi sylfeini'r byd;
Ti roist im yno drysor maith di-drai;
Gad imi heddiw gael dy wir fwynhau.
O cofia'r hedd rai prydiau roist i lawr
I'm henaid trist mewn cyfyngderau mawr;
O! edrych eto, mae fy enaid gwan
Gan syched mawr ar drengi yn y fan.

Nid rhaid it ond dywedyd gair o hedd
Fy syched a dry 'a dawel nefol wledd;
Fe dderfydd gofid, derfydd hyfedd wae,
Fy nhristwch lyncir yn dy wir fwynhau.[27]

(Forget not thy precious faithful Covenant, that was made firm before the world's foundations were laid; there thou hast given me a great unfailing treasure; grant me today to taste thy true joy. O remember the peace thou hast sometimes sent down to my sad soul in great tribulations; O look again, my feeble soul is near to death from its great weight. Thou needest but to speak a word of peace, and my drought will turn to a quiet heavenly feast. My pain will be ended, my sadness swallowed up in the true enjoyment of thee.)

III

In this chapter I have hoped to suggest three things. First that within the Christian tradition the relationship between the world of the Reformation, at least in its classical manifestations, and the world of Latin Catholicism and Eastern Orthodoxy, is much closer and more intimate than many people have supposed. Without glossing over genuine differences, we can see that at the level of faith and experience, there are great and significant areas held in common. In the field of spirituality there are things in the one tradition which require a knowledge of the others for their full understanding. Andrey Rublyov, John of the Cross, Williams Pantycelyn, are closer relations than we knew. All are blinded by the splendour of the one divine beauty, and all have used the resources of their art to convey something of it to us.

Secondly, it has been suggested that the study of theology, when carried on in the spirit of a scholar like von Balthasar, can engage in a fruitful conversation and collaboration with a variety of other disciplines. The study of Christian spirituality leads to a study of the forms of personal prayer and meditation, and that can very quickly bring us to the investigation of literary and poetic texts on the one side, and of the characteristics of the human psyche on the other, while the study of the more public and corporate forms of Christian worship links the study of theology with the history of the arts, music, architecture, painting and sculpture. In Eastern Christianity in particular, the icons provide vital clues to the understanding and interpretation of the Christian faith. A consideration of the whole range of the experience of Christian prayer and life, from the most exalted to the most earthy of its manifestations, can involve the theologian and the Church historian in a dialogue with historians and sociologists of many kinds, not to speak of the students of the other great religions of mankind.

But thirdly, I have hoped that what is written here might have a particular relevance to the situation of those who live in Welsh-speaking Wales as well as more widely. There are in this field of study very special possibilities and opportunities in places where two rooted and substantial linguistic and cultural traditions, in this case English and Welsh, live side by side. No one who cares about these matters can be unaware that there are pains and problems, agonies indeed, in a bilingual situation. But are there not also unrealized potentialities? There is in Welsh Wales a richness of experience and understanding in the interaction of the two traditions which is not open to those who live in other parts of Britain, let alone in other parts of the world, which have become monolingual. Should not the English-speaking majority, both in Wales and England, look again more deeply at the heritage of Wales, at the Welsh language itself with its abundance of words for beauty, excellence and splendour? There is a secret here which we have not yet understood, something hidden in the Welsh literary tradition with its astonishing resilience and sense of continuity. It is a tradition which has at its heart the practice of praise, praise of God's glory, God's beauty seen shining out in all the things of earth, a glory which calls men and women on through its celebration to a knowledge and a love which go beyond this world and touch on the world of eternity.

Diversity of Tongues: curse of Babel or gift of Pentecost

The subject of this chapter touches one of the basic themes of Bible and tradition alike; first, the fall of humanity and its subsequent disintegration, then the redemption of humankind and its subsequent fulfilment. The dispersion of Babel is balanced and corrected by the unity which Pentecost brings. This vision of a double movement finds classical expression in one of the Byzantine hymns for this feast,

> When the Most High came down and confused the tongues
> He divided the nations.
> But when he distributed the tongues of fire
> He called all to unity,
> Therefore with one voice we glorify the All Holy Spirit.[1]

But though the subject is a theological one, it is considered here in terms of the lived experience of Christian faith and prayer and life, in terms of the gifts of the Spirit, in terms, that is to say, of spirituality. The systematic study of spirituality as we saw in the last chapter is comparatively recent in the English-speaking world as a whole, but it is everywhere attracting greater attention and proving remarkably fruitful.[2]

One of its most evident advantages is that it encourages inter-disciplinary studies. By taking seriously the practice of prayer and meditation, for instance, it relates the study of theology to the study of literature; the poetry of meditation, whether in George Herbert, T. S. Eliot or R. S. Thomas, whether in Morgan Llwyd or Waldo Williams, demands this kind of convergent approach. The study of spirituality leads us to examine the inner life of humankind, our psychological and spiritual development. But it also considers the social consequences of belief, and thus touches on the sociology of religion. It seeks to see theology in relation to intellectual and cultural history as a whole. A remarkable example of such a study, though it does not use the word, can be seen in Derec Llwyd Morgan's work on the early stages of Welsh Methodism, published in English translation in 1988 as *The Welsh Revival*.

The study of spirituality necessarily also places Christian tradition in the context of the other religious traditions of mankind. There are few more promising ways of approach to the comparative study of religions than this, with its constant desire to link theory with practice and to trace the personal, social, political and cultural consequences of different patterns of belief. Within a specifically Christian context, the study of spirituality also combines the practical with the theoretical. Above all it goes hand in hand with a renewed concern for the doctrine of God the Holy Spirit, and hence for the doctrine of God as Trinity, for here we are concerned not only with the spirit of man, but with God as Spirit. To speak of God as Trinity is to affirm that at the heart of the Godhead there is relatedness, plurality, distinction as well as utter unity of being. It is to speak of God's love as a mystery which exists within the being of God from all eternity, a mystery which overflows into the creation and redemption of the world. And this, as we have seen in the previous chapter, is something which unites Christians of widely separated traditions.

This mystery of divine love touches men and women in their totality, in their personal and social being, in their heights as well as their depths, in body, mind and spirit. Its effect is cleansing, enlivening, transforming. It is by no means confined to our inner world, though it is certainly active there, nor is it confined to what has been called 'religious experience'. The study of spirituality resists any tendency to restrict the work of the Spirit to a purely religious sphere. That tendency has, it must be acknowledged, deep roots, particularly in the Christian west and not least in Anglicanism. We might think of the Catechism in the 1662 Prayer Book, which speaks of the work of God in terms of three concentric but diminishing circles, the Father who creates the whole world, the Son who redeems the whole of humankind, the Holy Spirit

who sanctifies the whole elect people of God. Rather the study of
spirituality will tend to think of the activity of the Spirit in the
more inclusive terms of the Byzantine prayer 'O Heavenly King,
O Comforter', which speaks of the Spirit as 'everywhere present
and filling all things'.

Such an affirmation of faith in God the Holy Spirit, as Lord and
life-giver, carries with it the thought of the Spirit as the source of
change and development in the creation, the origin of multiplicity
and diversity as well as of unity and order. This theme is insisted
on in the New Testament in a number of ways. At Pentecost
according to the Book of Acts there was a diversity of tongues. In
the letters of St Paul it is clear that the Spirit is at once the Spirit of
unity and relatedness, and the Spirit of diversity and differentiation. There are different gifts for each one. This Pauline
teaching is expressed in many ways in later Christian tradition, as
for instance in the eleventh-century Latin verse for Pentecost
which prays,

> Come, Holy Spirit, and fill the hearts of your faithful people
> and kindle in them the fire of your love; in the diversity of all
> tongues you have gathered together the nations into the unity
> of faith (*per diversitatem linguarum cunctarum gentes in unitate fidei
> congregasti.*) Send out your Spirit, Lord, and they shall be
> made, and you shall renew the face of the earth.

The unity which the Spirit brings is thus seen as a unity in
difference, a unity in freedom, which brings out rather than
suppresses the multiplicity, the richness of this universe which
God has made. It creates a qualitative rather than a quantitative
catholicity, a catholicity in which the whole is present in each
part. So Waldo Williams can write 'In me, Wales is one' (*Yn of mae
Cymru'n un*). We discover our uniqueness as persons in discovering
that we are totally one with all our fellow human beings in the
unity of our common human nature. As James Nicholas says, we
discover, 'the binding thread of the brotherhood of man, which is
also the thread of our freedom' (*Edau caeth brawdoliaeth dyn, edau ein
rhyddid wedyn*).[3] A Latin writer of the eleventh century, Peter
Damian, puts it thus,

> By the mystery of her inward unity [brought about by the
> action of the Holy Spirit], the whole Church is spiritually
> present in the person of each human being who has a share in
> her faith and brotherly love. So it is that that which belongs to
> all belongs to each, and conversely that which is particular to
> some is common to all in the unity of faith and love.[4]

This highly personalist view of the work of the Spirit in the
church and human society as a whole, has been strongly
developed by a number of modern Orthodox theologians, both
Russian and Greek, among them, Vladimir Lossky, Nicholas
Afanasieff and John Zizioulas. All in different ways have wanted
to articulate the deep conviction of Eastern Christianity about the
centrality of the work of the Holy Spirit in the life of the church
and of the world as giver of freedom and diversity as well as of
unity and peace. The same thoughts have begun to emerge more
powerfully in the west as theologians have been forced to think
more deeply on the nature of unity and catholicity in the course of
the present movement of convergence which is actually bringing
the separated Christian denominations into new relationships of
mutual understanding and exchange. It is significant that the
unity to which so many Christians look forward is never conceived
in terms of uniformity, rather in terms of a reconciled diversity.[5]

I

This vision of the work of the Holy Spirit at Pentecost as
diversifying as well as uniting finds splendid expression in the
hymns and sermons of N. F. S. Grundtvig (1783–1872), one of
the two great Danish theologians of the nineteenth century.
Grundtvig was a man who united a passionate concern for a
rediscovery of the true nature of his own people and their
language, with a no less passionate concern for a rediscovery of a
universal Christian vision. In terms of his own period he may be
seen as a romantic nationalist. It is significant that his name is
better known in Wales than in other parts of the British Isles,
precisely because of his influence on the early years of Welsh
nationalism, through the thought of D. J. Davies and Noelle

Davies. So far however the full scope of Grundtvig's vision has been very little appreciated in the English-speaking world, or indeed anywhere beyond his native country.

At Pentecost 1837 Grundtvig preached on the text 'We hear them speak in our own tongues the great and wonderful works of God.'

> Such an exclamation, he begins, was not unusual in ancient days, when the poets of every people, inflamed with invisible fire, spoke to them with winged words, in parables and in image language about the ones who dwell in the heavens, yet come down to consider the earth, and sometimes in a wonderful way, to visit the children of men, regarding them as their distant relatives, greatly impoverished and yet not wholly degenerate. It was not unusual, I say, for this happened not only in Israel, when the prophets spoke, but also amongst all the heathen, who had not altogether forgotten that humankind was originally one family with its creator. It is the creator who breathed the breath of life into man's nostrils, and placed the word in man's mouth, the word about the unseen world, the wonderful expression of thought and feeling and the stamp of deity, by which we can be distinguished from all creatures who do not speak . . . [6]

It is very striking that in this opening passage of his sermon, Grundtvig sees the event of Pentecost not as an isolated wonder, nor as something altogether without precedent in human history, but rather as the totally unmerited fulfilment of a divine activity which despite the fall has never ceased throughout creation. The Holy Spirit is everywhere present and filling all things. He makes of the human race a single family in God. He spoke clearly through the prophets and poets of Israel. His utterance in the prophetic figures of other nations may have been less clear, may indeed have been dark and confused, but it has never wholly ceased in the history of humankind. The longing to recover 'the ancient kinship of earth and heaven' (*Hen gyfathrach nef a llawr*), as Waldo Williams calls it, has always been there. Echoes of the divine Spirit have not ceased to resound in the spirit of man. Christian theologians and preachers have not always been so affirmative about the work of pagan poets and seers as Grundtvig is here. But this more positive evaluation of their vision has its antecedents in various parts of the Christian tradition, in Clement of Alexandria and the early apologists, for instance, in the Catholic humanists of sixteenth and seventeenth-century Spain, or in many of the poets of medieval Wales, who saw a close link between the *awen* (the poetic muse) and the Holy Spirit of God, and who gave a high evaluation of the work of *poets, makers*, those who create through the assistance of the Creator Spirit himself.[7]

Grundtvig develops his own thought about the relationship between the spirit within man and the creative, transforming Spirit of God, as the sermon goes on. This feeling of kinship between earth and heaven

> was not wholly foreign to any people who had a word in their mother tongue, which expressed what we call spirit, for in all languages this word is derived from the feeling that there is a strange, unseen power, which even less than our bodily breath can be investigated or described, but which, when it is active, puts us in a wonderful relationship with another, higher world. Yes, it opens up such a world in our own inmost being, in our mind and in our heart, so that we discover a whole world of new thoughts and feelings, not as something foreign to us, but as something which was fast asleep and almost dead, but which now awakens in us and begins, as it were, to draw breath. This is how it was when the apostles' hearers on that great feast of Pentecost exclaimed in amazement, 'We hear them speak in our own tongues, the great and wonderful works of God.' In this respect what happened to them is not something alien, but something altogether human, something which makes it clear that what is above nature in the church of Christ is in no way against nature, but rather the divine blessing and transfiguration of the deep and glorious, but deeply fallen and wounded nature of man, which it pleased our heavenly Father to raise up, to regenerate, to renew, bless and transfigure in his only begotten Son, the seed of Woman, our Lord Jesus Christ.[8]

It is remarkable that Grundtvig here insists that what the Spirit awakens within us is something deeply human, something of our own, something already there, 'that of God in every man', something deeply buried, fast asleep, almost dead, but none the less universally given. Pentecost touches the depths of our being, and although it is above nature, it is in no way against nature. It renews and transforms our humanity in its diversity and multiplicity. It is interesting to see how a contemporary theologian writing about the missionary activity of the church and the relationship of faith to culture, can make a very similar point in commenting on this same passage of Scripture. John D. Davies, speaking out of his own experience of the meeting of major and minor languages in southern Africa, and of the clash between dominant and international cultures on the one side, and threatened local cultures on the other can say:

> The miracle of Pentecost is not just that people are enabled to understand each other ... The point is made with considerable emphasis, that communication comes to them not in the international language of the powerful, but in the local languages of family, region, nation ... This is the heart of the miracle. Our own language, however insignificant in the eyes of the empire builders and the powerful advertisers, is claimed as a suitable vehicle for the good news ... Those who heard the apostles' words did not only get information about events external to themselves; they also got an assurance of their own value, through the affirming of the language which shaped their basic perceptions.[9]

The first language through which we have learnt to think and feel, remains inextricably bound up with our perception of the world and our perception of ourselves. To threaten to destroy it is to threaten our very identity as people and as a people. As John D. Davies points out the assault on the Afrikaans language by English educationists in the early part of this century is one of the basic factors lying behind the intransigence of the Afrikaner position today.

It is often said in Britain that the number of people speaking Welsh is now small. Such assertions need to be questioned. What is the content of the word 'small' in this context? There are languages among the Indian people of North America, for instance, which are spoken by no more than five thousand people, yet which are used in worship and education as well as in all the activities of daily life.[10] To enter into and share the language of so small a linguistic group is not only to affirm something about the unique and irreplaceable worth of the people who use it, it is also to be taken into a family relationship with that people, to be given a share of their whole experience of the world and its history. To enter into such a relationship is to understand something about the value and meaning of human life which is beyond any calculation conceived purely in terms of numbers and quantity. It is to discover something of the God-given richness of the diversity of humankind. This, which is true of the learning of a language spoken by a single tribe, is, in a similar way, true also of learning the language of a numerically small nation. Theologically speaking, the gift of tongues at Pentecost is precisely this affirmation of the importance and worth of human diversity against all tendencies to a monolithic or imposed uniformity.

II

This threat to the diversity of human society and culture is perceived at this time by people of very different standpoints and convictions as a threat to our very humanity. Its articulation is by no means always explicitly theological. It has been powerfully expressed by some twentieth-century writers and critics, not least by Jeremy Hooker, a critic remarkable for his perception and understanding of the meaning of particular places. For Hooker it is above all the poet who in our century is called to keep open these varieties of possibility within human life and experience. Following the example of Patrick Kavanagh he takes the word 'parochial' and seeks to give it a positive, affirmative meaning. In a published interview he says,

> I've come increasingly to see a function of the poet as re-expanding or attempting to contribute to the re-expansion and rediscovery of the world in which we live. I think one of the greatest threats to the twentieth century, which is symbolized as well as represented by the threat of nuclear

extinction, is that of sameness, uniformity, of seeing all things and all places as if they were one. But the parochial poet can help make the world larger again, and can help us to breathe, can help us to feel the reality of the world in which we live by dwelling upon the particular, by discovering or rediscovering the particular. I like to quote Roy Fisher, who wrote of Birmingham, 'Most of this has never been seen' ... We can help to return a sense of wonder to the world, a sense of vitality to existence, a sense of reality to place by seeing closely the places that we know and in which we live ... A great regard for the parochial, a great regard for the things of which the individual has been made in a particular place contains within it a respect for all places, and in that sense also the world is expanded. Drawing attention to the reality of any one particular place does something rather similar for all other places.[11]

The felt diversity of place of which Jeremy Hooker speaks here, is, one may suppose, a quality to be found in all settled, pre-industrial societies. But it seems to have been characteristic of the Celtic world to an outstanding degree. At many times and at different periods there seems to have been an intense sense of local loyalties, of the interpenetration of people and the places where they have lived. And because Celtic society has often been basically tribal, small units, geographically and numerically, have taken on a wealth of significance. This is one of the themes to be found, for instance, in Alfred Smyth's study of Celtic Leinster, which stresses the fact that the tribal kingdoms of Leinster, for all their smallness, supported an extremely rich cultural and religious life. The seventh century in particular saw the flowering of learning in their monastic communities, and 'for a region which supported such an intense pursuit of scholarship there is no other parallel in either the rest of the Celtic world or in Anglo-Saxon England'.[12] More than a millennium later in Nonconformist Wales we can find a similar flowering of literary and religious interests in places which from a metropolitan viewpoint seem marginal and insignificant. So a historian of the distinction of R. T. Jenkins can devote a whole book to the study of a single Independent chapel in north Wales.[13]

This sense of the rediscovery and re-expansion of particular places can be seen in relation to Ann Griffiths, whose whole life, as we have seen, was passed within the parish of Llanfihangel-yng-Ngwynfa and most of it within the single farmhouse, Dolwar Fach. It may be said that this is a very special case, an untypical moment of fervour and vision in the early years of the Methodist movement in north Wales. But we may think of the picture of another rural neighbourhood, another parish, painted more than a century later, when the first fire had passed from that form of religion as it became part of a whole way of life. I refer to D. J. Williams's portrait of the district in which he was brought up as we find it in *Hen Dŷ Ffarm*, in English, *The Old Farmhouse*.

This is indeed a portrait which rediscovers and re-expands for us that beloved district in such a way as to enrich and enlarge our vision of all other places. The religion of D.J.'s book is unobtrusive and unpretentious, woven so closely into the fabric of life as to be scarcely visible. Yet it is certainly there. Consider for a moment the care with which the writer tells us about the practice of family prayers, *y ddyletswydd*, in his childhood home.

> Between my grandfather and my father after him the family devotions were observed in Penrhiw and Abernant for over sixty years without a break. Moreover if I may suggest it in all humility, it is probable that this tradition if it could be traced, reached back to the old home in Llywele, and had come down from father to son from the conversion of Wiliam Sion, my grandfather's grandfather, in the beginnings of Methodism in the vicinity, a hundred years before the sixty I have spoken of.[14]

Here there is indeed the tracing of an apostolic succession.

Think again of what we are told about the writer's father.

> His nature had no trace of deceit or jealousy. His great gift was the gift of prayer. It was a joy to listen to him when he knelt . . . I think he was always on good terms with his Creator. I know that he was on the best terms possible with his neighbours, every hour of the day and every day of the year. That was a part of the secret of the life of the Old Neighbourhood.[15]

If what D.J. tells us of his father reveals part of the secret of the life of that place, what he says of his mother lets us still further into the secret. Here the prayer in question is not public but hidden.

> Very often when she was busy at her work without dreaming that anyone was listening, I would hear her chanting her prayers and meditations in a gentle, adoring monologue, weaving through them, in a beautiful way, psalms and verses of hymns . . .my mother did not speak much of her religion beyond praising the goodness she saw in others and being tender-hearted towards their weaknesses. It is my belief that her life, every minute of it as it came, was all one secret prayer.[16]

There is the hidden link between Penrhiw at the end of the nineteenth century and Dolwar Fach a hundred years earlier.

We find here the unseen source of that sense of the rediscovery, the re-expansion of the small, the forgotten, the inconspicuous, which marks all the writing of D.J. In the practice of prayer every minute can be touched by eternity, every place can be opened to the expanses of heaven. Seamus Heaney remarks on this when speaking of Patrick Kavanagh and his memory of the childhood prayer called the Morning Offering.

> I believe that the spirit of this prayer, the child's open-eyed attention to the small and the familiar, is fundamental to Kavanagh's vision, as is the child's religious belief that if each action, however small, is offered up for love, then in the eyes of God it is as momentous as the great, noisy, cataclysmic and famous acts which make up history.[17]

The destructive tendencies towards uniformity and sameness which characterize our time stem from a failure to see the eternal dimension present within each moment, the infinite possibilities present in each grain of sand. Too often, in our century, human life becomes entrapped, imprisoned within an iron reign of cause and effect; there is no room for freedom or creativity, no possibility of breathing the air of eternity. The practice of prayer and the faith which sustains it, create a sense both of the bonds which link the separated moments of time and space in the one communion of saints and also of the indefinite richness and diversity which mark each point in that coherent but complex unity.

It is this capacity for heightening our perception both of the unity and diversity within creation, and of creating within human society a communion in which differentiation is enhanced and not annihilated, which attracted one of the great Christian writers of our time, David Jones, to the Catholic faith. As Jeremy Hooker remarks,

> Christianity . . . is the one unifying force that David Jones, the poet who celebrates the unique individual differences born of the marriage between people and place, finds creative; and for him it is the principle of creativity. To each place its own genius, a genius deriving from the female creative principle, which the Catholic poet finds embodied in its highest form in the Mother of God. Christ is the Lord of order, but what he orders is personality, unique, individual things, which uniformity – military, technological or impersonal – tries to destroy. For David Jones the personality of Britain, that which because it is creative embodies the true nature of man, is intimately bound up with the fate of Wales. It is there, in the genius of place, that he sees the foundations preserved, which an increasing tendency towards uniformity obliterates.[18]

The truth of this observation about David Jones's understanding of the female creative principle is wonderfully borne out in his poem 'The Tutelar of the Place', in which Mary is addressed as,

> Queen of the differentiated sites, administratrix of the demarcations, . . .
> mother of particular perfections
> queen of otherness
> mistress of asymmetry
> patroness of things, parti, pied, several
> protectress of things known and handled,
> help of things familiar and small
> wardress of the secret crevices

of things wrapped and hidden
mediatrix of all the deposits
    margravine of the troia,
empress of the labyrinth . . . [19]

Mary in the infinite variety of her involvements with place, 'Our Lady of this, Our Lady of that', embodies in herself this qualitative catholicity which far from being opposed to outward catholicity is its safeguard and protection. In her we see that in creation as in the Godhead itself, identity and distinction, unity and multiplicity, are not in opposition to one another. She in a special way stands protectress over Wales. We might think in this connection of her place in the work of poets as diverse and unexpected as Gwili, Euros Bowen and Gwenallt, and it is Wales which holds the key to the preservation of the personality of Britain, *yr ynys hon*, whose true unity is precisely *not* a uniformity.

It was this perception of the vital place of diversity within the unity of humankind and the vital place of Wales within the unity of Europe, which lay behind the convictions which animated the founders of the Welsh Nationalist Party in the 1920s and 1930s. Their position has frequently been misunderstood and misrepresented. Our century has seen such an excess of destructive and exclusive nationalism that people have become reluctant to speak at all about the question of nationality. But in fact the resolutely international view of nationalism which inspired the beginnings of Plaid Cymru, and which finds its expression in its earliest manifesto, *Principles of Nationalism, Egwyddorion Cenedlaetholdeb*, is as much the enemy of a tyrannical or racist nationalism as it is of a bland, uniform internationalism. Nations like persons need one another, exist in relationship to one another, find themselves in their encounter with one another. There is nothing isolationist, let alone of the ideology of the master race, in the original formulations of Saunders Lewis.[20]

Saunders Lewis and his associates saw a close analogy between the person and the nation; each of them being a God-given, sacred and irreplaceable reality. In this view of the parallel between the two, the early Welsh nationalists owed much to the thought of Jacques Maritain, as Dafydd Glyn Jones has pointed out in his masterly essay on Saunders Lewis's political thought. The nation, like the person, needs to respect the rights of others; but it has its own rights which also need to be respected.[21]

It is interesting that this line of thought has received powerful expression in some of the dissident writing which came from the Soviet Union, writing which is the more impressive in that it was undertaken in the face of all kinds of totalitarian pressures. In the volume of essays edited by Solzhenitsyn, entitled *From Under the Rubble*, the historian Vadim Borisov writes on the subject of 'Personality and National Awareness'. For him, as for Maritain, the distinction between 'person' and 'individual' is of vital importance. The person 'is not a part of some whole, it comprehends the whole within itself'. Individuals may be thought of as replaceable units, numbers, heads, cogs within a machine. Persons are irreplaceable and unique. We may destroy them, only God can create them. As with persons so it is with nations. Only where there is a living memory can the identity either of persons or nations be maintained. 'A necessary precondition of a people's existence and development is historical memory.'[22] Solzhenitsyn himself in his Nobel Prize speech follows a similar line of thought. He speaks of literature as being 'The living memory' of a nation. 'Literature together with language preserves the national soul', he declares, and goes on to affirm

> the disappearance of nations would impoverish us, not less than if all men were to become alike, with one personality and one face. Nations are the wealth of mankind, its generalised personalities; the least among them has its own unique coloration and harbours within itself a unique facet of God's design.[23]

It seems as though the impact of communism in the countries of eastern Europe has aroused in many of them a strong sense of the significance of national identity. It is a theme which is to be found in many places in the writing of Pope John-Paul II. With his own remarkable linguistic gifts, with his keen sense of the value of his own mother tongue and of its links with the other Slavonic languages, the Pope has shown himself particularly perceptive in this area. For him, the unity of the church is a unity in diversity,

requiring the eastern no less than the western tradition. At the
cultural level the unity of Europe is also a diversified one, Slavonic
as well as Latin, Celtic as well as Germanic and Anglo-Saxon.[24]

III

We come back to our initial question, *Diversity of Tongues, Curse of
Babel or Gift of Pentecost?* If in this chapter we have stressed the
aspect of gift and blessing rather than of curse, that is because the
first and negative aspect of our subject hardly needs to be
emphasized. It is not easy for different languages and different
cultures to live together in the same society. Diversity of tongues
can be a source of suspicion and misunderstanding, division and
hostility. We do not have to look further than Belgium to see some
of the problems of a state which contains two sharply dif-
ferentiated linguistic groups. If we look to the new nations of
Africa we see still more clearly the dangers involved in tribal and
linguistic divisions. Yet even at the political level, there are other
and more hopeful examples. Switzerland, for instance, shows us
the possibility of respecting and encouraging linguistic minorities.

And if, as we have argued, a positive evaluation of the diversity
of this world and human society within it, is an integral part of a
Christian vision of things, then surely it is the duty of the churches,
in Britain and Ireland to take a more active role than they usually
do in the affirmation and development of the linguistic and
cultural diversity which characterizes these islands. That is a
diversity which is in part very ancient, the diversity of England,
Scotland, Wales and Ireland. It is a diversity which is in part very
modern, the result of movements of immigration which have
taken place during the last generation. We need a theological
reflection on these developments in order to respond actively to
the faithless and destructive despair of Enoch Powell and his
supporters. This can come from a vision of the world as made by
God in diversity as well as unity, from a vision of a qualitative
catholicity of life, which respects and does not destroy human
differences and variety. This means that we need not only a
bilingual but a multilingual policy not only in Wales, but in
England, not only in England but in Scotland and Ireland.

This will involve for all of us, but particularly for the great majority of us who are monoglot English-speakers, very radical changes of attitude which strike at the linguistic habits of fourteen hundred years. We need to recognize, for instance, how strange it is that in English education so little place should be given to the history and tradition of the peoples who for all these centuries have been our closest neighbours. There are very deeply ingrained habits of mind which prevent us from seeing how extraordinary it is that there is not a single university in England where one could study the post-Reformation language and literature of Wales, and that it is regarded as abnormal rather than normal for an educated English person to have even a modicum of knowledge of Welsh. Such facts point to a degree of blindness which is disabling indeed, an unwillingness to recognize the existence of the other and to let him speak in his own terms, which, while it is universal in our fallen humanity, is yet a special affliction of peoples with an imperial past. I have no doubt that this century-old failure of recognition, of *adnabod*, is closely linked with our current inability to meet the most recent strangers to arrive in our midst and to understand them in their own terms. The inability of the British government to hear what was being said by the tragic events in places like Handsworth, Brixton and Tottenham was ultimately rooted in our age-old English refusal to hear and learn the languages of others, and in particular of our western neighbours. The ancient history is linked with the new. A deep and genuine change in English attitudes towards Welsh could be, I believe, an important pre-condition for a more human, more sensitive, more constructive approach to the urgent problems of our multi-cultural inner city areas.

If we are to make that new approach we need to find a new vision. We shall find at least some vital elements of it not only in the act of learning Welsh but also in the discovery of what is to be found in the poetry of the last fifty years. There we find a remarkable achievement of Christian affirmation, to which the fierce lucidity of Saunders Lewis, the sympathetic penetration of Waldo Williams, the sacramental affirmation of Euros Bowen have all contributed. Perhaps in the context of our search for a qualitative rather than a quantitative catholicity we shall find it above all in the work of Gwenallt, a poet of international and ecumenical stature whose significance has as yet hardly begun to be recognized. For Gwenallt the principle of the incarnation is to be seen at work in all things. That means that the universal and the particular for him are always held together. He had a vision of the church as at once Catholic and local, rooted and free. As Idris Foster puts it, 'In his later poems Gwenallt's precise, as-a-matter-of-fact naming of persons and places – it is an old feature of Welsh poets – is particularly noticeable'.[25] The exactness of his topography is fused with the universality of his vision.

It was his fear that Rome still hankered after an imperial uniformity which prevented him from becoming a Roman Catholic. It was the same perception which made him withdraw from the communion of the Church in Wales at a time when he thought that that church in the person of some of its highest officers, was indulging in a piece of similar if less justified imperial arrogance. It is this vision of a complex but organic unity of human and divine, of temporal and eternal, of local and universal which finds expression in the great poem written in memory of J. E. Daniel,

> Clymu dyneiddiaeth y Dadeni wrth ddiwinyddiaeth
>   Drindodaidd,
> A gosod diwinyddiaeth yr Eglwys yng nghanol
>   argyfwng Cymru.
> Clymu Caersalem ac Athen a Bangor.

(He tied the humanism of the Renaissance to the theology of the Trinity, and placed the theology of the Church in the midst of the crisis of Wales. He linked Jerusalem and Athens and Bangor.)

We find this same theme in two other poems from his last collection, *Y Coed,* namely 'Swper yr Arglwydd' and 'Catholigrwydd' (The Lord's Supper and Catholicity). In the former we are present at a service of Holy Communion in the great church of Llanbadarn Fawr. The mystery of the incarnation made present in the Eucharist is expressed in striking images, Mary wrapping up God's infinity in a napkin, and rocking eternity to sleep in his cradle. The need in the church both for continuities of time and space, as well as for the descent of the Holy Spirit, is suggested in the verse which speaks of the sound of running water in an Italian city square and also of the enveloping bonfire of Christ's divine humanity. But it is in 'Catholicity' that Gwenallt makes his most explicit statement on this subject, a statement of faith in the qualitative catholicity of the church, in the power of the Spirit who descended at Pentecost to make a unity which brings together separated places and people into a unity which does not destroy but which fulfils them, indeed which brings together human and divine into precisely such a unity of love.

He was imprisoned by his flesh and Jewish bones within the confines of his land, but he gave them as a living plank to the hammering and was raised from the grave in spite of the guard, as a Catholic body by his Father. And now Cardiff is as near as Calvary, and Bangor every inch as near as Bethlehem. Storms are stilled on Cardigan Bay, and in every street the afflicted find healing from the touch of his hem. He did not hide his Gospel among the clouds of Judaea, beyond the tongues and eyes of men, but he gives the life which lasts forever in a drop of wine and a crumb of bread and the gift of the Spirit in the flow of water.[26]

The Knowledge which Unites: the death-defying quality of art

The comparison of one art form with another, music with sculpture for instance, is always a risky business. To make a comparison between verse and painting, as we intend to do here, between a strict Welsh verse form and the Eastern Orthodox tradition of painting icons might seem an altogether unnecessary risk, particularly since the very existence of a contemporary literature in the Welsh language is so little known outside Wales, and so has been the subject of very little comparative study. But we have already found the comparison of the churches of sixteenth-century Moldavia, with the hymns of eighteenth-century Wales an illuminating one, and so we propose in this chapter to go further along this line, to attempt to see how icons and *cywyddau* can illuminate one another, how two traditional and public art forms, even if coming from widely separated parts of the world, can have something vital in common, which makes their comparison surprisingly fruitful.

One of the few facts about contemporary Welsh verse which is sometimes known outside Wales is that it employs strict metres which date from many centuries ago. It is interesting to note that there has been a distinct revival in the use of such metres during the last twenty years; a flourishing periodical entitled *Barddas* has been produced particularly devoted to work of this kind.[1] The quality of such writing can be, one may suppose, very variable. But even the humblest kinds of verse-making ought not to be despised. It is in the soil of many undistinguished acts of composition that great poetry can take root and flourish. And where old techniques and conventions of versifying persist as living realities, it proves possible to do and say things which are no longer possible when such traditions have ceased to exist. Form cannot be separated from content. What can be said is to a considerable extent dependent on the way in which it is said. The persistence of the old metres is one of the factors which has made possible the explicitly religious affirmations of much modern Welsh poetry, affirmations which contrast strongly with the indirectness of language which even a profoundly theological poet like T. S. Eliot feels bound to employ when treating such themes in English.

Amongst these verse forms is the *cywydd* (Englished in the seventeenth century as *cowith*), not by any means the oldest of them, but certainly amongst the most exacting.[2] It was the vehicle of much of the finest writing of the golden age of Welsh poetry, the period from 1350 to 1500. It was used most brilliantly by the greatest of all poets of that time, Dafydd ap Gwilym; in fact it was possibly even invented by him. It was a new metre, free from the heroic associations of the older forms used by the poets of the princes before the fall of the last Welsh Prince of Wales in 1282. It could be employed for a variety of lighter and more personal themes, the vicissitudes of love, the celebration of nature, petitions to a patron, elegies for the departed. One of the qualities which marks the whole Welsh tradition is a desire for a kind of epigrammatic terseness, a desire to say much in little. In the *cywydd* this quality is emphasized by the shortness of the lines, only seven syllables long, and by the fact that even they are divided into two halves and constructed with intricate patterns of internal alliteration and assonance. This is what is called *cynghanedd* in Welsh, a technique which Gerard Manley Hopkins described as 'consonantal chime'.

In a special number of *Poetry Wales* devoted to work in the strict metres and published in the summer of 1978, the editor, J. P. Ward, remarked,

> The tight form, used successfully, seems to be insisting that the poet emphasise a certain feeling very deeply by making all the words he chooses practise a certain self-denial in reinforcing that feeling. It is almost as though – and this does not at all deny the tremendous facility with which some poets do this —

the words are forced into position against their will, and this,
paradoxically, makes them strain like bent metal, giving
them great tension and power. It makes each different line or
phrase seem to belong to and be contained by some over-all,
hidden idea binding it.[3]

In such writing, form and content are inseparably bound
together. As the English poet Harold Morland who knows Welsh
put it, in the same number of *Poetry Wales*, *cynghanedd* is

cunning in the way it strings
on stirring sounds a strong sense.

Here we begin at once to see the similarities between the *cywydd*
and the icon. The icon painter, too, accepts a very strict set of
conventions which enables him to achieve the special effect which
he wishes for. He too forces his lines to practise a certain self
denial, so that the whole picture may become the vehicle of some
'over-all hidden idea binding it'. Here too we are conscious of a
concentration of energy and meaning. There is in the icon great
power and tension expressing itself through great and only
apparently effortless calm and serenity.

But here also we see one of the most striking differences between
the icon and the *cywydd*. The icon is an explicitly liturgical art
form. It is made within a given tradition of faith and worship,
painted with prayer, to be used with prayer, corporate or personal,
to be used as a sacramental vehicle through which the grace and
power of the Kingdom of Heaven can come to the worshipper,
and through which the praise and adoration of the worshipper
may mount to the heavenly realm. The place of the icons within
the church building and the way in which the icons are related to
one another, are both things which are controlled by strictly
theological criteria. Those who have written about the meaning
of icons in the last forty years have rightly stressed the gulf
which separates them from other kinds of religious painting in
which the artist simply expresses his own feelings in relation to
some incident from the Bible or church history. In iconography
the artist is the servant of the tradition. He seeks to efface himself,

so that through the offering of his prayer and skill, the given truth of the Gospel of God may shine out in all its beauty.

Now the *cywydd* has never had this explicitly and exclusively theological function. Dafydd ap Gwilym uses it for satire and farce, for describing the joys of summer, or the delights of illicit love, and this is the practice of innumerable poets since. Here is a great and undeniable difference. But despite this fact, the similarities remain, for behind and through all the uses to which the metre has been put, there is in Welsh an underlying understanding of the purpose of poetry as praise, and at its ultimate point, as praise of God. It was the very certainty of the Christian structure of medieval life and thought, which made it possible to include everything, even the most apparently incongruous elements, in a form which has its origins in praise and prayer. As Anthony Conran, one of the most expert of translators of Welsh poetry, put it, in the same number of *Poetry* Wales, 'Whereas the surface is often expressionistic and idiosyncratic, the core is almost always the agreed nature of poetry as praise'. The liturgical function is there in the background, and the whole way in which the poet's work is understood in Wales to this day, as a public as well as a personal act, as being in some sense a service to a whole people, has an unmistakably liturgical flavour to it. The *cywydd* is not a specific form of sacred art, but it comes from a time when the inherent 'sacredness' of all forms of art was more generally acknowledged than it now is, implicitly if not explicitly, and it can convey something of that quality still today.

I

The two poems which we shall be discussing in this chapter, both come from our own century and not from the Middle Ages. In both we see that this 'agreed nature of poetry as praise' is explicitly affirmed. They are elegies for dead poets, icons of masters of the craft; and they are the work of two deeply believing and theologically perceptive writers who, in their celebration of friends and teachers now dead, are able to affirm something of the power of God given to man to overcome death. In them, as in the icon, the death-defying quality of all true artistic creation becomes explicit. For it is important to recognize that while the icon is distinct from other forms of painting, secular or religious, it proclaims aloud something which is implicit in all true forms of human creativity. In all of them there is the desire to affirm meaning and understanding, to express the splendour of form and the permanence of beauty, in the face of the powers of meaninglessness and death which always threaten human life. The specific forms of sacred art, icon-painting or plain-chant for instance, though clearly distinct from other less directly God-directed forms of art, are not unrelated to them. The baffled longings for immortality which we find in all forms of artistic making are not only judged but fulfilled by the Gospel of Christ's triumph over death through death. Hence the importance of the icon which proclaims the triumph of life, human and divine, for all forms of artistic endeavour.

In the ninth century, St John of Damascus could speak of the icon as 'a song of triumph and a revelation, and the enduring monument of the saints', those in whom God's love has been at work, who display the power of the risen Christ to overcome all that frustrates and binds down the life of man. The icons contain a very strong affirmation of the continuing relationship of the present with the past, of the saints on earth with the saints in heaven, in and through the life of God which is stronger than death. But these affirmations have an analogy in the death-defying quality inherent in all true making. In the poems which we are about to examine this analogy becomes very clear. Just as the one who has departed this life comes to meet us in his icon, so too in these poems the dead whom they celebrate come out to greet us.

The first of these two *cywyddau* is the work of Waldo Williams (1904–71), one of the best-loved figures of twentieth-century Wales, and a poet of great distinction.[4] It is in this context interesting to notice that he came to have a particular admiration for the writings of the Russian theologian Nicholas Berdyaev. The poem is addressed to E. Llwyd Williams, a close friend who died in 1960, himself a fine poet and for many years a Baptist minister in Rhydaman. The second of our two poems is an elegy addressed to Waldo himself, and is the work of James Nicholas, one of the most renowned of writers in the strict metres of our own day.[5] Both poems begin by confronting death in one of its most shattering forms, the death of the poet, the maker. They confront the destruction of the 'God-given and God-like ability in man to create (and all fine creation is *ipso facto* an attestation of the divine, an act of worship)',[6] in other words they confront the possibility of the annihilation of the very image and likeness of God in man. Both furthermore are written in a language which is threatened with extinction, a threat which indeed hangs over every language, but which is not usually perceived with the painful clarity which is to be found in Welsh-speaking Wales today. But both poems confront the fact of death within a tradition of faith and poetic technique which declares that by the death of Christ death itself has been destroyed, and that through the offering of the cross the life-giving Spirit is made free to work in the spirit and mind of man. Waldo begins like this:

> Where is the whole language if Llwyd is dead?
> Sentence is but a dream
> Or a cold mist on a barren heath
> If meaning has perished between us.

Meaning (*ystyr*, in Welsh, a word which derives from *historia*) exists between men in the use of language as a vehicle for the sharing of love and knowledge. As H. G. Gadamer puts it

> language has its true being only in conversation, in the exercise of understanding between people . . . All forms of human community of life are forms of linguistic community; even more they constitute language.[7]

Hence the whole language is threatened by the death of those who speak it, especially by the death of the poet, who is the maker, the guardian of meaning. At once the appeal to God follows:

> Pure God, Father of light,
> Give back to us your dawn.
> Your glory is your heart.
> Love springs up from your holy root.
> Above our clay your love binds us in one.

> You join us together, safely, above the fall.
> Dwell in us through this parting
> And bring our journey into the one House.

We are held together in death, and through death by the love
and power of God, which unites us above our clay. The fall of man
is a fall into death, into a state of separation from God and from his
fellow man. The God of Light gives us back the dawn, the dawn
alike of creation and resurrection. He gives it from his heart,
which is his love. It is this love which is his glory, *Dy galon yw
d'ogoniant* (Your glory is your heart.) The conciseness of the Welsh
is untranslatable; but we might say that the whole of the fourth
gospel's insistence that it is in the cross that God's glory is
revealed, the whole of later Catholic meditation on the meaning
of the heart of Jesus as the place of the divine love, is summed up in
this remarkable line. From the heart of God there comes the glory,
the love which fills heaven and earth, and which touches all things
under the earth. It is this which brings us to the house where are
the many mansions.

James Nicholas's poem 'Poet' begins with an even stronger
assertion of our sense of loss:

> The night of God around David's land,
> Silent is the voice, heavy the flood.
> Where is the heart, with its sea of light?
> Where is the one great bard who gives us life?
> Where is the hidden meaning of the master of song?
> O youth, where is the passion?

It is important to know in this poem that both its writer and the
one to whom it is written come from the same region of south-west
Wales, from Pembrokeshire, and have been much at St Davids,
the little cathedral town which lies at the western extremity of
that region, one of the holiest places of Britain. They are members
of David's family. They feel a deep kinship not only with one
another but also with the remote past which becomes so
powerfully present in that remarkable place. But this sense of
presence is a fragile, precarious thing. Death stills the poet's voice;
the waters of forgetfulness flood over us. The night of God's

absence swallows us up. The heart with its sea of light, the poet with his life-giving word, are gone. Where is the hidden meaning of the master of song? There is such perfection in the *cynghanedd* of this line as to be visible even to the non-Welsh reading eye. *Mae ystyr cudd y meistr cerdd?* The fact of death threatens all life, all meaning, all understanding, with destruction. 'Who can deliver me from the body of this death?' asks St Paul. No one, replies much in our twentieth-century culture. Meaninglessness and absurdity seem to rule over human life. But even from within the world of human culture another voice makes itself heard. The very possibility of our being able to hear and understand across the gulf of the centuries, across the gulf of death, our capacity to respond to works from ages other than our own tells us, as Gadamer puts it, that 'the duration of the power of a work to speak directly is fundamentally unlimited', it points to 'an element of ultimate community and sharing' in the world of meaning and understanding. This element of community and sharing is part of what in theological terms would be spoken of as the communion of saints. It tells us of a living tradition. In the light of Christ's resurrection we can affirm that man was not made to be the sport, the plaything, of death. He cannot be satisfied with a life totally hemmed in by space and time. The poet's art is, in itself, a witness against mortality.

> Even now the greatness
> of the poet's tongue breaks through the gate of death.
> His song brings him back.
> The feast is eternal.

And at once the poet goes on to recognize the origin of this power.

> Your muse was God's gift
> Strong from the root to rise up;
> Old, very old is this gift –
> This gift to unite men –
> It is the heart, the well spring
> Of all life, creating a better world.

Once again the character of the *cynghanedd* can become evident
even when the language is only guessed at. *Dawn Duw oedd d'awen
di* (your muse was the gift of God) *Hen, hen iawn ydyw'r ddawn hon*
(old, very old is this gift), the gift of the Word which reconciles, of
the Spirit which interprets. This certainly is the gift of Pentecost,
which unites mankind in the diversity of tongues. But has this gift
ever been wholly absent from the life of man? Has God ever left
himself without witness? Through all the ages has not the Creator
Spirit brooded over the chaos of human life, made himself known
in creation and redemption? What is the relation of the poet's
muse, his inspiration, to this inspiration of God the Spirit, the life-
giver? The poet does not resolve the many questions which arise.
He makes the basic affirmations of faith and experience which
make it possible and meaningful to ask them.

And then he goes on, in lines which are full of allusions to the
work of the poet he is celebrating, to speak of the way in which
men are called to live together as one.

> This is the gift, the thread
> Which we find being woven around us,
> The binding thread of the brotherhood of man
> Then to become the thread of our freedom.

The original of the last two lines again demands to be quoted,

> Edau caeth brawdoliaeth dyn
> Edau ein rhyddid wedyn.

The word *caeth* which has been translated 'binding' has its roots
in *captivus*. We are bound together in the web of humankind in a
binding which can enslave us in all the restrictions of our fallen
human state, unless we find through the gift of the Spirit that by
recognizing our unity of nature with all our fellow men, we are
able to receive our total and unique freedom as persons in a
relationship. 'When you see the naked cover him, and hide not
yourself *from your own flesh.*' (*Isaiah*) You shall love your neighbour
as yourself. This gift of the Spirit which is eminently social, which
creates human community, has its roots in what is most deeply

personal and inward, in the way in which we are enabled to love and to know. It is the gift of the knowledge which unites.

All around us we see the devastation caused by loves which become possessive and exploitative, and by ways of knowing which seek to subject and control. But these are a perversion of the true nature and destiny of humankind. In the power of the Spirit men and women can know and love in such a way as to unite and not divide, to give life and not to take it. Only in the gift of the Spirit do we find that unity which respects and preserves all the diversity of creation, only in him do we find the power which enables us to recollect and to remember; and as Heidegger maintains that is the essential characteristic of all true knowing. For before it involves analysing, distinguishing, dividing, knowledge implies in-gathering, harvesting, uniting.

The poet goes on to affirm this very thing of the departed master. He knew understanding, *Hwn a wybu Adnabod*, a line which depends for its effect on the existence in Welsh of two verbs for 'to know', one corresponding to the French 'savoir', *gwybod*, scientific knowledge, the other corresponding to 'connaître', *adnabod*, personal knowledge, recognition, understanding. This term *adnabod* is one of the keys to understanding the life and work of Waldo. He indeed knew this knowledge, which is a knowledge in love and reconciliation, in mutual sharing and participation.

> He knew understanding
> Which is the core of living and the root of being
> From the one root the roots branch out
> And the goodness of the tree is lasting.
> How alive is the root,
> The depth of God is the riches of man.

Gwaelod Duw yw golud dyn, again a line in which the 'consonantal chime' seals and establishes the meaning in all its complexity and richness. 'The depth of God is the riches of man'. The abyss of God's love, the design of God's love from all eternity, these are indeed the unending riches of man who is made in God's image, rooted and grounded in the creative love and understanding of his Creator. And although the word *gwaelod*, depth or foundation,

does not have the meaning of descent, the thought that the depth
of God's love is revealed in his emptying himself and taking the
form of a servant, in his going down into death, even the death of
the cross, can not be far away from this line. By becoming poor he
makes many rich. By coming to be with us he raises us to be with
him. By accepting death into himself, he overcomes death and
gives us his life. *Gwaelod Duw yw golud dyn.* The depth of God is the
riches of man. It is a statement which, for richness of implication,
may remind us of the words of Irenaeus, *Gloria Dei homo vivens; visio
Dei vita hominis.* The glory of God is a living man; the life of man is
the vision of God.

Both the poems at which we have been looking begin on a note
of questioning and anguish. Both end on a note of serenity, with a
strong sense of presence and of gift. Both end with the image of
night, for in this life we walk by faith and not by sight. We do not
here have any fullness of vision, any fullness of knowledge, when
we stand before the mystery of death. But the darkness of the night
is full of stars.

'The grove of night is full of heaven', writes Waldo. *Llawn o Nef
yw Llwyn y nos.*

> In it is your muse tonight,
> May its grace shine out, encompass the land.

James Nicholas ends

> Good night, favour of Dewi;
> The poet is heaven's gift to us.

These lines contain words of Christian and liturgical resonance
which it is particularly difficult to translate. The word which I
have rendered as 'grace' means privilege, honour, the dignity and
worth which God gives to his human creatures, and which we
receive from God. The word which I have translated as 'favour'
means kindness, generosity or condescension. Again it suggests
the freedom of God's action. The poet is the gift of God, and the
gift of God's saint. He reveals and incarnates the descending,
redeeming love of God. Waldo's poem ends with the prayer that
through the poet's work, God's generosity may shine out and

spread through the land, the *bro*, the known and loved neighbourhood, a word which means much in terms of the intensely
local loyalties of Wales. It is a word which needs today to be
interpreted more widely in a planet which has suddenly become a
single neighbourhood.

II

Even in translation perhaps something of the quality of these two
particularly untranslatable poems has become evident. In them
we see the truth of David Jones's comment about Welsh poetry in
general, that the form and the content, the sound and the
meaning, are inextricably at one. They are works certainly not
notably typical of the spirit of the age we live in. They make direct
statements about God and his goodness; they praise with
simplicity, and feel no need for defensive or apologetic irony. Like
the icon, to which we come back, they speak with the confidence
and authority of a tradition which is living today but which has its
roots in another age, or better, in an eternal world which
transcends and informs every age. The writers are conscious of
acting in an area in which the idea of the muse, of inspiration, is no
mere convention. Waldo Williams declared in a lecture given in
English, one of his rare statements in our language, 'We can never
tell how far our life is lived for us by the unconscious nor how far
meaning is meant for us'. In works such as these the tradition from
which they come speaks out, the spirit in which that tradition lives
shines forth. This meaning is both something given and received.
In this way, like icons, the poems become epiphanies, manifestations of an eternal glory.

Like icons, too, these poems are also representations of real,
flesh-and-blood people. There is little enough direct description in
James Nicholas's poem about Waldo, but the references to St
Davids, and the multiple allusions to Waldo's own writings,
firmly anchor it in the life and work of a particular man. In
Waldo's own poem there are clearer specific references to the life
of his friend, to the place where he lived, to the members of his
family who are left behind. He speaks of his work as a minister of
the Gospel, 'He gathered in an imperishable harvest.'

These references remind us of the details often included in the icon of a saint which tell us that here we have a representation of a historical being, not an imaginary vision of some ideal figure. This anchoring of the icon in the flesh and blood of a particular man or woman is of the utmost importance. It points us to the particularity of the incarnation itself. Of course the poems do not give us a naturalistic description of the men they acclaim, nor does the icon give us a detailed naturalistic portrait. It shows us this particular man in relationship to God, as one in whom the divine Light shines out. It shows us the serenity and fullness of heaven in and through the limitations and constraints of earth. It opens up a window on to an eternal realm, constituting a 'calculated trap for meditation', a prismatic glass through which we may catch sight of things otherwise invisible. In particular the icon invites us to enter in and share in the reality which it portrays. This is the meaning of the reversed perspective which the painter uses, which projects the figures towards us. This, too, is the reason why the saints are always depicted looking directly at us, coming out to meet us. When we stand in front of an icon we are not as in an art gallery, simply spectators, even if deeply interested ones. We are called to become participants in what we see and to learn through our participation.

The same is true, in ways appropriate to the medium they employ, of the poems we have been considering. They are not primarily didactic, any more than the icon is primarily didactic, but in the poems, no less than in the paintings, there is an invitation to life, and a celebration of God's gift of life. After the publication of his only volume of poems, *Dail Pren* (*Leaves of the Tree*), Waldo Williams declared, 'I hope that *Dail Pren* will be of *practical assistance* to my nation amid the confusion of this age'. His hope has surely been realized. The poems have been, and are, of practical assistance in the business of living. Like icons they renew our courage to be. In particular they celebrate the art of the poet as an art which reconciles and unites, as a divine gift which makes human community possible. In Waldo's poem this is made explicit in the close association of Llwyd's work as a minister of the Gospel, with his work as a master of song. In his gentle and open-hearted concern for his fellow human beings, we see a parallel to his care for language itself, the means by which understanding and mutual confidence become possible.

> He was a shepherd of shining countenance,
> A good servant always seeking understanding,
> Leading the one into the confidence of the other,
> into that fullness which knows no ending,
> The husbandry of God's neighbourhood.

The Johannine references are inescapable. To dwell in love is to dwell in God. As we are gathered together into our small congregation of Christ, wherever it may be (here the Baptist congregation of Rhydaman), as we learn truly to know and love the particular people with whom we share our daily life, so we find ourselves gathered together into an eternal company. The work of the minister no less than of the poet is a work of in-gathering, of harvesting, it is the husbandry of God's neighbourhood. In him we see the fulfilment of man's calling to be, like his Maker, 'the shepherd of being'.

And so by the living and not merely imitative use of traditional forms the concentrated expression of centuries of experience is made possible. The poems shine like jewels, like enamelled miniatures with that same condensation of meaning which we recognize in the icons. In both cases the artist must be at once highly disciplined and self-effacing; he uses great self-denial so that an eternal reality may be disclosed. All this does not happen by chance, nor without the exercise of human freedom and skill and creativity. It is done through the carefully acquired mastery of inherited techniques, through the infinitely sensitive handling of paint and wood, of sound and meaning. A contemporary Russian scholar, Nicholas Zernov, says of icons, 'they are dynamic manifestations of man's spiritual power to redeem creation through beauty and art . . . pledges of the coming victory of a redeemed creation over a fallen one'.[9] In this he rightly stresses the role which men and women must play in offering their creative powers to take their part in the divine-human work of creation and redemption. We find here an expression of the Russian Orthodox understanding of our call to be a co-creator with God, and we note with interest that this idea was developed with particular force by Nicholas Berdyaev, a thinker who, as we have noted, greatly impressed Waldo Williams. But this power of free creativity is itself the Spirit's gift and in both the icons and the *cywyddau* which we have been considering it may well be the sense of the transcendent gift and generosity of God which strikes us most, the gift of the life-giving Spirit won for us through the death on the cross, by which death is destroyed and life is made free; won for us also by the artist's own willingness to 'die to self' so that the work of art which he is making may come to life.[10]

We remarked earlier in this chapter that for the poet writing in Welsh today the possibility that his language may be extinguished can never be altogether absent from his mind. This gives a particular sharpness to his perception of the nature of language itself. Just as in Constantinople in the last two centuries before 1453 the makers of mosaics and the painters of frescos seem to have received some special capacity to celebrate the Lord of life in face of the constant threat of death to their city, so too in our own unpropitious age the Christian poets of Wales have received the gift to sing of the beauty of creation and of God's glory revealed in all that he has made, with a kind of God-given exhilaration. Their work shows a courage and a joy which contrasts strongly with the surrounding gloom of so much twentieth-century culture. Very characteristically, Saunders Lewis, the greatest of them all, declares,

> You say we're for the dark, that our language is doomed? All right my bonny, be it so – and how long is your own expectation of life? At any rate we, here in Wales, will make it the end of a lovely party, leaving great verse unto a little clan.[11]

For of course, by all human calculations, all our languages are in the end doomed to die. Men and nations are none of them immortal. All must in the end go the way of Etruscan; unless indeed our feeble lights are held in God's eternal light, our brief memories sustained in the memory of one in whom love and knowledge are alike eternal and life-giving; *Sub specie aeternitatis*, our only hopes of overcoming death are found in him.

But in a much shorter term view of things we may at least reflect on this. Sixty years ago it would have been impossible to have written this chapter, not so much because the two poems with which it is concerned had not been written – there were plenty of other *cywyddau* to examine – but because the icon as a liturgical art form was unknown in the western world, except to the occasional specialist in the history of Byzantine art. In sixty years the situation has changed entirely. Everywhere in the west, icons are appreciated and admired. In an increasing number of places they are coming to fulfil their true purpose as vehicles of prayer, sacraments of the meeting between earth and heaven. In a variety of ways the tradition of Orthodoxy is spreading in the west, as a lived and known reality. Who knows but that in another sixty years the *cywydd* and the tradition which it represents could be equally well known, admired and appreciated throughout the English-speaking world? Who knows but that the language and heritage of the people who for 1,500 years have shared the island of Britain with the English will no longer be a closed book to the millions who have English as their mother-tongue? The hidden meaning of the masters of song is to be known more widely, the gift which these poems convey is to shine out further into the world and to be of practical assistance, not to one nation only, but to many in the gathering in of an imperishable harvest.

Epilogue

The pages of this book have unfolded a great and varied affirmation of the splendour of God revealed in his creation. It is an affirmative statement of a kind which is rare in our twentieth century, when the poets and playwrights, the novelists and film-makers have more often chosen to show the dark side of human existence, its brutality, its absurdity, its ultimate nothingness, than its potential for glory and joy. This dark side has of course been present in the Welsh tradition too, particularly in its element of satire and polemic. We can see it clearly in our own century in the work of men like Gwenallt and Saunders Lewis, not to speak of more recent writers.

But within the Christian tradition of prayer and praise, it has always been recognized that there is need for another and still more profound question mark to be placed against such statements of affirmation. There is a way of negation of images which is a necessary complement and corrective to the way of affirmation, a way of negation which in the end goes even further. Unless we remember that the God to whom all names apply is also the God who is utterly beyond all names, *innominabile* as well as *omninominabile*, the words which we use about him will tend to become too definitive and limiting, too closed and literally understood. There is a danger that we shall become too comfortable in our affirmation of God's glory seen in the face of his creation, that we shall take ourselves and our words too seriously, too literally, and lose sight of the immeasurable inadequacy of every part of the created universe to represent fully the infinity of its Creator. Then our words and concepts will become solid objects in themselves, idols which imprison us, rather than windows or doorways which open out a way for us beyond all words and images into the silence, the mystery, the infinity, the nothing of the divine being. For God is indeed *no thing* that we could comprehend or say in any final or definite way.

This radical refusal of concepts and images, this way of going to God beyond all words and concepts, this determination to say of him, 'not this', 'not that', has its greatest statement in the early Christian centuries in the writings of the sixth-century Syrian author known as Dionysius the Areopagite. Having written a treatise on the divine names, Dionysius goes on to write another on mystical theology; the knowledge of God in a silence which is more than words, a darkness which is more than light; the deep but dazzling darkness of which Henry Vaughan and many others speak. This way is taken up again in the spiritual writers of the medieval west, in England by the author of *The Cloud of Unknowing*, and on the continent by writers such as Ruysbroeck and Tauler, Suso and above all Meister Eckhart. In the poetry of twentieth-century Wales, it has been followed by R. S. Thomas, one of the outstanding writers in English. Much in this book could be read as providing a background to the understanding of his work.

But in writing in Welsh, this dark, corrective side of the Christian affirmation was never far from the surface of the mind of the writer with whom we began our whole enquiry, Saunders Lewis. It is with him that we must end. The poem which follows is one which caused great controversy and great distress at the time when it was published in 1973. At first sight 'Prayer at the End' appears highly negative. Was the writer as he grew older denying the faith which he had spent so much of his life expounding and defending?

> It is the experience of all which no one else knows about.
> Each one for himself and in his own way
> Owns his own death,
> Through the millions of years of our race.
> We can look on, sometimes we can recognize the
>   moment;
> No one can feel with another in that moment
> When the breathing and the person come to an end.

Afterwards? There is no reaching to afterwards except
    in the groping of our prayer.
How poor is man, how childish his imagination.
'In my Father's house are many mansions',
As poor as ourselves, his genius as limited
In the days of his self-emptying.
And we can only picture our hope in the same way
'Seated at the right hand of God the Father Almighty,'–
Commander in chief with his triumph through the city
    of Rome
After the awfulness of a Persia of a creation
Crowned as Augustus, Co-Augustus with his Father,–
How comic are the highest definitions of our faith.
And around us is the silence, and the pit of nothingness
Into which our whole universe will fall one night.
Our words cannot at all contain that silence
Nor say God with meaning.
One prayer remains to all, to go silently to the silent.

Saunders Lewis himself commenting on these lines in the controversy which followed the publication of the poem wrote,

> Is not our language, are not our images, our talk about 'sitting at the right hand', necessarily and pitifully 'comic'? How can we with the language which is ours be equal to such things? We are human beings, comic little creatures; there is not much difference between us and mice. But there are some of us who dare to believe that God became man.

In his discussion of the poem Saunders Lewis refers us to the fourteenth-century mystics of Germany and the Low Countries.

> I only know them through quotation and extracts, and I should be ashamed if anyone thought I was an expert in them. But their teaching about prayer has opened my eyes and is part of the influence on the vocabulary used in these lines.

In such writers it is possible to speak of the silence, the nothingness of God, to recognize that we can say nothing directly about God at all. We have to go to God through the discipline of silence and the discipleship of prayer. And following Morgan Llwyd, amongst the post-Reformation writers of Wales, Saunders Lewis suggests that this way of silence and darkness in prayer is itself a kind of death, a dying to our own light, our own life, our own understanding. Thus he declares death itself may be like a prayer, a prayer at the end.

The glory which the Christian poet seeks to embody and declare is the paradoxical glory revealed in its fullness in the self-giving of the cross. The life and love which he celebrates is a mystery which is wholly gift, and never wholly our possession. As the ninth-century master declares of God's glories 'no words can contain them, no letters can express them'. As Ann Griffiths saw so clearly we have to come out of our own 'ceiled houses', the little world of our own ideas and imaginings, if we are to enter into the dwelling-places of the Three in One. In creation and redemption alike, God's glory goes beyond all that we can think or say. A thousand years earlier a biblical writer had exclaimed

> To put it in a word, he is all. Where can we find the skill to sing his praises? For he is greater than all his works.' (Ecclus.43[28])

Notes

Foreword

1. 'The Essence of Welsh Literature' in Alun R. Jones and Gwyn Thomas (eds.), *Presenting Saunders Lewis* (Cardiff, 1973), 155–6. The paragraph contains an allusion to Francis Thompson's lines, 'Thou canst not stir a flower/Without troubling a star'. See R. S. Thomas, *Pe Medrwn Yr Iaith* (Abertawe, 1988), 145.

2. Thomas Parry in his note to this poem in *The Oxford Book of Welsh Verse* (Oxford, 1962), 555.

Chapter 1

1. David Jones, *Epoch and Artist* (London, 1959), 281.

2. Joseph P. Clancy, *Medieval Welsh Lyrics* (London, 1965), 4.

3. Quoted in Aneirin Talfan Davies, *Dylan, Druid of the Broken Body* (London, 1964), 1.

4. Philip Toynbee, *End of a Journey, An Autobiographical Journal 1979–1981* (London, 1988), 84.

5. Les A. Murray, 'Embodiment and Incarnation; Notes on Preparing an Anthology of Australian Religious Verse', *Eremos Newsletter, Occasional Essay Supplement*, January 1987 (Sydney, 1987), 6–7.

6. Waldo Williams, *Dail Pren* (Aberystwyth, 1956), 43.

7. Giolla Brighde MacCon Midhe, 'A Defence of Poetry', in Thomas Kinsella (ed.), *The New Oxford Book of Irish Verse* (Oxford, 1986), 98–102.

8. Ifor Williams, *The Beginnings of Welsh Poetry* (Cardiff, 1972), 102. There is a discussion of the problems of the manuscript here. The translation is slightly adapted.

9. Enid Pierce Roberts, *Hen Eglwys Y Cymry* (Bangor, 1988), 34–5.

10. Joseph P. Clancy, *The Earliest Welsh Poetry* (London, 1970), 113.

11. *The New Oxford Book of Irish Verse*, 53–4.

12. Thomas Merton, *Bread in the Wilderness* (London, 1954), xi.
13. Ibid., 49.
14. Ibid., 54.

Chapter 2

1. Theodore Chotzen, *Recherches sur la poésie de Dafydd ab Gwilym* (Amsterdam, 1927), 178.
2. See, for example, Joseph P. Clancy, *Medieval Welsh Lyrics* (London, 1965), 49–50.
3. Tony Conran, *Welsh Verse* (Bridgend, 1986), 175–6. The original poem 'Trafferth mewn Tafarn' can be seen in Thomas Parry (ed.) *Gwaith Dafydd ap Gwilym* (Cardiff, 1952), 327–9.
4. Ibid., 65.
5. Ibid., 176–7. The original poem 'Y Ceiliog Bronfraith' can be seen in T. Parry (ed.), ibid., 81–2.
6. Dafydd ap Gwilym, *A Selection of Poems*, edited by R. Bromwich (Llandysul, 1982), 74–6.
7. John Gower, *Miroir de l'Omme* ll.5632ff.
8. For the study of Edmwnd Prys, the vital work is Gruffydd Aled Williams, *Ymyrson Edmwnd Prys a Wiliam Cynwal* (Cardiff, 1986).
9. Gwyn Jones (ed.), *The Oxford Book of Welsh Verse in English* (Oxford, 1977), 81–3.
10. Thomas Charles and Thomas Jones (eds.), *Trysorfa Ysprydol* 1799–1800, (Caerlleon), 160. I am grateful to my friends Dr Oliver Davies and the Revd Paul Quinn for help with the translations of Thomas Jones.
11. On this poem see Saunders Lewis, *Meistri a'u Crefft* (Cardiff, 1981), 87–96 and Bobi Jones, *Llên Cymru a Chrefydd*.
12. Thomas Parry (ed.), *The Oxford Book of Welsh Verse* (Oxford, 1962), 332–9.

Chapter 3

1. Gwynn ap Gwilym and Alan Llwyd (eds.), *Blodeugerdd o Farddoniaeth Gymraeg yr Ugeinfed Ganrif* (Llandysul, 1987).
2. D. Gwenallt Jones, *Ysgubau'r Awen* (Aberystwyth 1939), 85.
3. Bobi Jones, *Selected Poems*, translated by Joseph Clancy, (Swansea, 1987), 104. The original poem 'Bardd Llys' can be seen in Bobi Jones, *Tyred Allan* (Llandybie, 1965), 66.
4. Joseph P. Clancy, *Twentieth Century Welsh Poems* (Llandysul, 1982), 190–1.

The original poem 'Y Berth' can be seen in *Cerddi'r Llanw* (Llandybie, 1969), 37–8.

5. Ibid., 158–9. The original poem 'Llanddwyn' can be seen in Pennar Davies, *Y Tlws yn y Lotws* (Llandybie, 1971), 56.

6. Gwynn ap Gwilym and Alan Llwyd (eds.), ibid., 71–2.

7. Bobi Jones, op. cit., 63. The original poem 'Bwyta'n Te' can be seen in Bobi Jones, *Tyred Allan* (Llandybie, 1965), 9.

8. Euros Bowen, *Detholion* (Cardiff, 1984), 199.

9. Tony Conran, *Welsh Verse*, 279.

Chapter 4

1. Joseph P. Clancy, *Twentieth Century Welsh Poems* (Llandysul, 1982), 96–7. The origianl poem 'Ar Gyfeiliorn' can be seen in D. Gwenallt Jones, *Ysgubau'r Awen* (Aberystwyth, 1939), 28.

2. Gwyn Thomas, *Living a Life, Selected Poems*, edited by Joseph P. Clancy (Amsterdam, 1982), 66–8.

3. Ibid., 86–7. The original poem 'Y Ffatri'n Cau' can be seen in Gwyn Thomas, *Symud y Lliwiau* (Dinbych, 1981), 61.

4. Tony Conran, *Welsh Verse*, 290–1. The original poem 'Wedi'r Canrifoedd Mudan' can be seen in Waldo Williams, *Dail Pren* (Llandysul, 1956), 90.

5. D. Gwenallt Jones, *Eples* (Llandysul, 1951), 63–4.

6. Alun R. Jones and Gwyn Thomas (eds.), *Presenting Saunders Lewis* (Cardiff, 1973), 182–3.

7. D. M. and E. M. Lloyd, *A Book of Wales* (London, 1953), 269–70.

Chapter 5

1. The Welsh original of this lecture, 'Ann Griffiths: Arolwg Llenyddol' is to be found in Saunders Lewis, *Meistri 'r Canrifoedd* (Caerdydd, 1973), 306–18. The English translation is in *Homage to Ann Griffiths* (Penarth, 1976), 15–30. For a general introduction to Ann Griffiths see A. M. Allchin, *Ann Griffiths: The Furnace and the Fountain* (Cardiff, 1987). The quotations from her work in this chapter are from that book.

2. Laurens van der Post, *Jung and the Story of our Time* (London, 1976), 270.

3. Ibid., 125.

4. Op. cit., 308 and 17.

5. Quoted by Saunders Lewis in his BBC lecture *Tynged yr Iaith* (1962),

to be found in English translation in Alun R. Jones and Gwyn Thomas (eds.), *Presenting Saunders Lewis*, (Cardiff, 1973), 131 and 133.

6. R. Tudur Jones, *The Desire of Nations* (Llandybïe, 1974), 147–8.

7. John A. Newton, *Search for a Saint: Edward King Bishop of Lincoln* (London, 1977), 14.

8. Morris Davies, *Cofiant Ann Griffiths* (Dinbych, 1865), 56.

9. Ibid., 57.

10. 'Y Santes Ann' in *Cofio Ann Griffiths* (1805–1955) (Caernarfon, 1955), 9.

11. T. S. Eliot, *Murder in the Cathedral* (London, 1935), 87.

12. *Homage to Ann Griffiths*, 12 –13.

13. Ibid., 13.

14. Dyfnallt Morgan (ed.), *Y Ferch o Ddolwar Fach* (Nantperis, 1977).

15. Gordon Rupp, *Just Men* (London, 1977), 33.

16. William Wordsworth, *The Prelude, 1805 version* Book IV, ll.341–4.

17. Thomas McFarland, *Coleridge and the Pantheist Tradition* (Oxford, 1969), 161.

18. An excellent account of the frescos is to be found in Wilhelm Nyssen, *Bildgesange der Erde: Aussenfresken der Moldauklöster in Rumänien* (Trier, 1977).

19. Romul Joanta, *Roumanie, Tradition et Culture Hésychastes* (Paris, 1987), 21.

Chapter 6

1. Thomas Kinsella (ed.), *The New Oxford Book of Irish Verse* (Oxford, 1986), 3.

2. T. S. Eliot, *Four Quartets* (London, 1944), 36–7.

3. R. S. Thomas, *Welsh Airs* (Bridgend, 1987), 53–5.

4. For the history of the plygain see Gwynfryn Richards, in 'Y Plygain', *Journal of the Historical Society of the Church in Wales*, Vol I No. 2 (1947), 53–71.

5. Enid Pierce Roberts, 'Hen Garolau Plygain', *Transactions of the Honourable Society of Cymmrodorion*, (1952), 51–70.

6. Gwynfryn Richards, art. cit., 66–7.

7. R. M. Jones (ed.), *Blodeugerdd Barddas o'r Bedwaredd Ganrif ar Bymtheg* (Llandysul, 1988), 118–19.

8. Geraint Vaughan-Jones, *Hen Garolau Plygain* (Talybont, 1987), 41.

9. Gwynfryn Richards, art. cit., 65.

10. Geraint Vaughan-Jones, op. cit., 29.

11. H. A. Hodges, in *Homage to Ann Griffiths*, 12.

12. Geraint Vaughan-Jones, op. cit.

13. David Thomas (Dafydd Ddu Eryri), *Corph y gaingc* (Dolgellau, 1810). The first of the two verses quoted comes from this work, 101. The second comes from a different source. Dafydd Ddu in the same carol speaks of a way being opened into the heavenly land, 'by the free, beloved Physician'. The image of Christ the Healer is common in the Welsh hymns and carols.

14. The ecumenical celebration of the Eucharist during the course of the Ann Griffiths festival at Dolwar Fach at the end of August 1989, might be seen as the beginning of such a public recognition.

Chapter 7

1. Alexander Solzhenitsyn: *Critical Essays and Documentary Materials* edited by J. B. Dunlop, R. Haugh, A. Klimoff (New York, 1975), 559.

2. Ibid., 560.

3. The full English translation of the *Philokalia* has now reached Volume III. There are two more volumes to come.

4. Hans Urs Von Balthasar, *The Glory of the Lord, a Theological Aesthetics*, Vol. 1 *Seeing the Form* (Edinburgh, 1982), 18–19. All seven volumes of the work are now available in English.

5. Saunders Lewis, *Meistri'r Canrifoedd* (Cardiff, 1973), 313. In the original the form of knowing described is that of the angels in which the contemplative participates.

6. G. M. Roberts, *Y Pêr Ganiedydd, Pantycelyn* (Aberystwyth, 1949), Vol. I, 83.

7. von Balthasar, op. cit., 125–6.

8. Ibid., 56.

9. This subject is admirably dealt with in Olivier Loyer's great but little-known work *L'Anglicanisme de Richard Hooker* (Lille/Paris, 1979). See especially the section entitled, 'Man as a Being whose End is God himself', 355–82.

10. John Keble (ed.), *The Works of Richard Hooker* (Oxford, 1895), Vol. I, 255–6. (Laws of Ecclesiastical Polity I,XI 3).

11. Ibid., 261–2 (L.E.P. 1 XI.6).

12. Ibid., 261 (L.E.P. 1 XI.6).

13. Ibid., 212 (L.E.P. 1 IV 1).

14. Op. cit., 39.

15. C. S. Lewis, *English Literature in the Sixteenth Century excluding Drama* (Oxford, 1954), 452.

16. *Llyfr Emynau a Thonau y Methodistiaid Calfinaidd a Wesleaidd* (Caernarfon, 1929), No. 589.

17. Glyn Tegai Hughes, *Williams Pantycelyn* (Writers of Wales Series, Cardiff, 1983)

18. G. M. Roberts, *op. cit.*, 167–8.

19. This quality of the Methodist movement in Wales has been admirably described by Professor Derec Llwyd Morgan in his major work *Y Diwygiad Mawr* (Llandysul, 1981), and in his more recent study of Pantycelyn in the series *Llên y Llenor* (Caernarfon, 1983). *Y Diwygiad Mawr* has been translated to English under the title *The Welsh Revival* (London 1988).

20. R. Tudur Jones, 'Rhyfel a Gorfoledd yng Ngwaith William Williams, Pantycelyn', in J. E. Wynne Davies (ed.), *Gwanwyn Duw, Diwygwyr a Diwygiadau* (Caernafon, 1982) 143–63.

21. *Emynau a Thonau* No. 681.

22. See Thomas Hancock, in A. M. Allchin, *The Spirit and the Word* (London, 1963), 54.

23. *Emynau a Thonau* No. 92.

24. *Emynau a Thonau* No. 390. The whole poem from which this verse comes is to be found in R. M. Jones, *Blodeugerdd Barddas o'r Bedwaredd Ganrif ar Bymtheg*, 257–9.

25. Metropolitan Antony (Bloom) in a lecture given at the Conference of the Fellowship of St Alban and St Sergius, at High Leigh in August 1984.

26. Op. cit., No. 390.

27. Ibid., No. 638.

Chapter 8

1. See Kallistos Ware, *The Orthodox Way* (London, 1979), 125–6.

2. The publication of *A Dictionary of Christian Spirituality* G. S. Wakefield (ed.) in 1983, and of *The Study of Spirituality* C. Jones, G. Wainwright and G. Yarnold (eds.) in 1986, are signs of the growing interest in this field.

3. T. Gwynn Jones (ed.), *Cerddi '74*, 66.

4. Peter Damian, *Selected Writings on the Spiritual Life*, translated by P. McNulty (London, 1959), 63.

5. The formula of 'reconciled diversity' is one which has been explored in the meetings of the International Lutheran-Roman Catholic Commission.

6. C. Thodberg (ed.), *N. F. S. Grundtvig's Praedikener* (Copenhagen, 1985), Vol. X, 224–5.

7. For Spanish sixteenth-century humanism see Ernst Curtius, *European Literature and the Latin Middle Ages* (London, 1953), 244–5 and 552–3.

8. N. F. S. Grundtvig, op. cit., 225–6.

9. J. D. Davies, *The Faith Abroad* (Oxford, 1983), 22–3.

10. For instance, the Nishga people in the Naas Valley in northern British Columbia. Information from the Very Revd J. C. Blyth.

11. Susan Butler (ed.). *Common Ground: Poets in a Welsh Landscape* (Bridgend, 1984), 204.

12. Alfred P. Smyth, *Celtic Leinster: Towards an Historical Geography of Early Irish Civilisation* (Dublin, 1982), 94–5.

13. R. T. Jenkins, *Hanes Cynulleidfa Hen Gapel Llanuwchllyn* (Bala, 1937).

14. D. J. Williams, *The Old Farmhouse* (E.T. London, 1961), 225–6.

15. Ibid., 224.

16. Ibid., 142–4.

17. Seamus Heaney, *Preoccupations: Selected Prose, 1968–1978* (London, 1980), 142.

18. Jeremy Hooker, 'The Poetry of David Jones', in *Poetry Wales*, Vol. 6 No. 3 (Winter 1970), 10.

19. David Jones, *The Sleeping Lord* (London, 1974), 62.

20. Saunders Lewis, *Canlyn Arthur* passim.

21. Alun R. Jones and Gwyn Thomas (eds.), *Presenting Saunders Lewis* (Cardiff, 1973), 40ff.

22. Alexander Solzhenitsyn (ed.), *From under the Rubble* (London, 1975), 194–228.

23. Alexander Solzhenitsyn, *Critical Essays and Documentary Materials* (New York, 1975), 566.

24. See in particular the Encyclical *Slavorum Apostoli*, issued to celebrate the work of St Cyril and St Methodius, apostles of the Slavs and inventors of the Slavonic alphabet.

25. Idris Foster, 'Review of *Y Coed*' *Poetry Wales*, Vol. 5 No. 3 (Spring 1970), 53.

26. Gwenallt, *Y Coed* (Llandysul, 1969), 26.

Chapter 9

1. *Barddas*, edited by Alan Llwyd.

2. For the origins of the cywydd see *A Guide to Welsh Literature* Vol. II,

edited by A. O. H. Jarman and Gwilym Rees Hughes, (1976), especially the chapters by Ceri Lewis and Rachel Bromwich.

3. *Poetry Wales*, Vol. 14 No.1 (Summer, 1978), 3–4.

4. The original with an English translation is to be found in R. Gerallt Jones (ed.), *Poetry of Wales 1930–1970*, 203–5.

5. James Nicholas's poem was published in *Cerddi '74*, edited by T. Gwynne Jones. I am indebted to my friend the Revd John Walters for introducing me to this poem and helping with its interpretation and translation.

6. Words of Colin Wilcockson on David Jones, in the same number of *Poetry Wales*, 135.

7. H. G. Gadamer, *Truth and Method* (New York, 1975), 404.

8. Ibid., 258.

9. Nicholas Zernov, *The Russians and their Church* (London, 1946), 108.

10. An even more moving icon/cywydd is to be found in Waldo Williams's tribute to his mother, *Angharad*, again an intensely original work. *Dail Pren*, 43.

11. Alun R. Jones and Gwyn Thomas (eds.), *Presenting Saunders Lewis* (Cardiff, 1973).

Epilogue

1. Gwynn ap Gwilym and Alun Llwyd (eds.), *Blodeugerdd o Farddoniaeth Gymraeg yr Ugeinfed Ganrif*, 75. For the comments see 602–3 in the same volume.

Books for Further Reading

In English

Meic Stephens (ed.), *The Oxford Companion to the Literature of Wales* (Oxford University Press, 1986).
Thomas Parry, *A History of Welsh Literature* (Oxford University Press, 1962).
Gwyn Jones (ed.), *The Oxford Book of Welsh Verse in English* (Oxford University Press, 1977).
Tony Conran, *Penguin Book of Welsh Verse* (Penguin, 1967), reprinted by Poetry Wales Press in 1986.
Joseph Clancy, *Medieval Welsh Lyrics* (Macmillan, 1965).
Joseph Clancy, *The Earliest Welsh Poetry* (Macmillan, 1970).
Joseph Clancy, *Twentieth-Century Welsh Poems* (Gwasg Gomer, 1982).
R. Gerallt Jones, *Welsh Poetry 1930–1970* (Christopher Davies, 1976).
Alun Jones and Gwyn Thomas (eds.), *Presenting Saunders Lewis* (University of Wales Press, 1973).
Derec Llwyd Morgan, *The Welsh Revival* (Epworth, 1988).
A. M. Allchin, *Ann Griffiths: the Furnace and the Fountain* (University of Wales Press, 1987).

In Welsh

Thomas Parry (ed.) *The Oxford Book of Welsh Verse* (Oxford University Press, 1962).
R. M. Jones (ed.), *Blodeugerdd Barddas o'r Bedwaredd Ganrif ar Bymtheg* (Barddas, 1988).
Gwynn ap Gwilym and Alan Llwyd (eds.), *Blodeugerdd o Farddoniaeth Gymraeg yr Ugeinfed Ganrif* (Gwasg Gomer/Barddas, 1987).
R. M. Jones, *Llên Cymru a Chrefydd* (Christopher Davies, 1976).
Pennar Davies, *Rhwng Chwedl a Chredo* (Gwasg Prifysgol Cymru, 1966).
Saunders Lewis, *Meistri'r Canrifoedd* (Gwasg Prifysgol Cymru, 1973).
Saunders Lewis, *Meistri a'u Crefft* (Gwasg Prifysgol Cymru, 1981).
Saunders Lewis, *Ati, Wŷr Ifainc* (Gwasg Prifysgol Cymru, 1986).
Dyfnallt Morgan (ed.), *Y Ferch o Ddolwar Fach* (Gwasg Gwynedd, 1977).

Index